THE IMPORTANCE OF

Louis Pasteur

by
Lisa Yount

Lucent Books, P.O. Box 289011, San Diego, CA 92198-9011

These and other titles are included in The Importance Of
biography series:

Alexander the Great	Galileo Galilei	Sir Isaac Newton
Muhammad Ali	Stephen Hawking	Richard M. Nixon
Napoleon Bonaparte	Jim Henson	Louis Pasteur
Rachel Carson	Harry Houdini	Jackie Robinson
Cleopatra	Thomas Jefferson	Anwar Sadat
Christopher Columbus	Chief Joseph	Margaret Sanger
Marie Curie	Malcolm X	John Steinbeck
Thomas Edison	Margaret Mead	Jim Thorpe
Albert Einstein	Michelangelo	Mark Twain
Benjamin Franklin	Wolfgang Amadeus Mozart	H.G. Wells

Library of Congress Cataloging-in-Publication Data

Yount, Lisa,
    Louis Pasteur / by Lisa Yount.
        p. cm.—(The Importance of)
    Includes bibliographical references and index.
    ISBN 1-56006-051-4 (acid-free paper)
    1. Pasteur, Louis, 1822-1895—Juvenile literature.   2.
Science—History—Juvenile literature.   3. Medical
sciences—History—Juvenile literature.   4. Scientists—
France—Biography—Juvenile literature.   [1. Pasteur, Louis,
1822-1895.   2. Scientists.   3. Microbiologists.]   I. Title.
II. Series.
Q143.P2Y68   1994
509'.2—dc20   93-49486
[B]   CIP
                                                           AC

TO STU AND GERI
Like Pasteur, hard workers and great family people

Contents

Foreword

THE IMPORTANCE OF biography series deals with individuals who have made a unique contribution to history. The editors of the series have deliberately chosen to cast a wide net and include people from all fields of endeavor. Individuals from politics, music, art, literature, philosophy, science, sports, and religion are all represented. In addition, the editors did not restrict the series to individuals whose accomplishments have helped change the course of history. Of necessity, this criterion would have eliminated many whose contribution was great, though limited. Charles Darwin, for example, was responsible for radically altering the scientific view of the natural history of the world. His achievements continue to impact the study of science today. Others, such as Chief Joseph of the Nez Percé, played a pivotal role in the history of their own people. While Joseph's influence does not extend much beyond the Nez Percé, his nonviolent resistance to white expansion and his continuing role in protecting his tribe and his homeland remain an inspiration to all.

These biographies are more than factual chronicles. Each volume attempts to emphasize an individual's contributions both in his or her own time and for posterity. For example, the voyages of Christopher Columbus opened the way to European colonization of the New World. Unquestionably, his encounter with the New World brought monumental changes to both Europe and the Americas in his day. Today, however, the broader impact of Columbus's voyages is being critically scrutinized. *Christopher Columbus,* as well as every biography in The Importance Of series, includes and evaluates the most recent scholarship available on each subject.

Each author includes a wide variety of primary and secondary source quotations to document and substantiate his or her work. All quotes are footnoted to show readers exactly how and where biographers derive their information, as well as to provide stepping stones to further research. These quotations enliven the text by giving readers eyewitness views of the life and times of each individual covered in The Importance Of series.

Finally, each volume is enhanced by photographs, bibliographies, chronologies, and comprehensive indexes. For both the casual reader and the student engaged in research, The Importance Of biographies will be a fascinating adventure into the lives of people who have helped shape humanity's past and present, and who will continue to shape its future.

Important Dates in the Life of Louis Pasteur

Pasteur is born December 27 in Dôle, France. — **1822**

1846-1848 — Graduates from Ecole Normale Supérieure; becomes doctor of sciences; researches crystals and discovers molecular asymmetry.

Begins teaching at University of Strasbourg; meets and marries Marie Laurent.

1849 — Begins fermentation studies while teaching at Lille.

Publishes work on lactic acid fermentation; returns to Paris and becomes director of scientific studies and administrator at Ecole Normale. — **1855**

1857 — Publishes work on alcoholic fermentation; conducts experiments on spontaneous generation and germs in air from different places.

1860

Discovers microbes that can live without oxygen; researches vinegar making. — **1861**

1863 — Researches diseases of wine.

1864

Gives lectures and demonstrations disproving spontaneous generation. — **1865** — Begins research on silkworm diseases.

1866

Publishes work on wine, including pasteurization process for preserving liquids by heating. — **1868** — Suffers stroke resulting in partial paralysis on left side; moves to larger laboratory.

1870

Publishes work on silkworm diseases; Franco-Prussian War. — **1871** — Begins research on beer.

1877

Begins research on anthrax. — **1878** — Studies childbirth fever and other human diseases.

1880

Discovers vaccine for chicken cholera; begins research on rabies. — **1881** — Trial of anthrax vaccine at Pouilly le Fort; Pasteur awarded Great Ribbon of Legion of Honor; elected to French Academy of Letters.

1885

Begins treating humans with rabies vaccine. — **1888** — Pasteur Institute opens.

1892

Great celebration of Pasteur's seventieth birthday. — **1895** — Pasteur dies at Villeneuve l'Etang on September 28.

Scientist of the Wonderful Century

In 1899 biologist A.R. Wallace wrote a book called *The Wonderful Century*. He credited twenty-four basic advances in science and technology to the nineteenth century. He claimed that only fifteen such advances had taken place in the entire earlier history of humankind.

Wallace may have exaggerated, but not by much. Nineteenth-century inventions include photography, railroads, the telegraph, and the telephone. Nineteenth-century scientists found ways to control electricity and chemical reactions. Science improved many people's standard of living and made European nations wealthy and powerful. It is not surprising that the time period is called the "Age of Progress." By the end of the century, most Europeans were optimistic about the future. They believed that life would improve as long as science and technology continued to advance.

Pasteur in His Time

In many ways, Louis Pasteur was a typical scientist of the "Wonderful Century." Like other nineteenth-century scientists, he stressed the importance of testing and proving ideas by experiment. He also used science to solve practical problems. He devoted much of his research to the needs of farmers and factory owners. His discoveries saved millions of francs (French currency) for makers of wine, beer, and

Louis Pasteur's scientific solutions to problems that plagued local industry made him a hero in the eyes of farmers and factory owners.

In and Beyond His Time

In Louis Pasteur: Free Lance of Science, *René Dubos describes Pasteur's impact on his own time.*

"Scientists, like artists, unavoidably reflect the characteristics of the civilization and the time in which they live. . . . A few of the greater ones, however, have visions that appear to be without roots in their cultural past and that are not readily explained by direct environmental influences. . . . Yet even they are not freaks in the natural sequence of cultural events. They constitute mentalities through which emerge . . . social undercurrents that remain hidden to less perceptive minds. Some of these visionaries succeed in converting their preoccupations . . . into messages and products of immediate value to their fellowmen; they become the heroes of their societies. Others perceive the hopes and the tasks of the distant future . . . but their anticipations are usually not understood by their contemporaries.

Pasteur belongs in both classes. As a representative of nineteenth-century bourgeois [middle-class] civilization, he focused much of his scientific life on the practical problems of his time. But as a visionary he saw beyond the needs and concerns of his contemporaries; he formulated scientific and philosophical problems that were not yet ripe for solution."

vinegar and for raisers of silkworms, chickens, sheep, and cattle. "There are not two kinds of science—practical and applied," he said. "There is only Science and the applications of Science, and one is dependent on the other, as the fruit is to the tree."[1] Pasteur's studies, like the work of most other nineteenth-century scientists, were not aimed simply at understanding nature. They focused on controlling other living things in order to protect or help human beings. The usefulness of Pasteur's research helped to make him the ideal nineteenth-century representation of what a scientist should be.

Pasteur's strong nationalism was also typical of the nineteenth century. He felt great love for and pride in France. He devoted much of his science to advancing French interests. "If science knows no country, the scientist has one, and it is to his country that he must dedicate the influence that his works may exert in the world," he said.[2] He also felt strongly, as did others in his time, that a country's strength was closely tied to its success in scientific research. He once claimed that "science is the highest personification of the nation."[3]

Changing Scientific Thought

Though Pasteur was a typical nineteenth-century scientist in some ways, in other respects he was a revolutionary who changed nineteenth-century thinking. At a time when only a few biologists studied microorganisms, or living things too small to see without a microscope, his "germ theory" showed that these tiny creatures had immense power to either help or harm humans. (*Germ* means "seed," but the word also came to mean "microorganism." After 1878 the term *microbe* was also used for microorganisms.) At a time when doctors blamed disease mostly on changes in the body, Pasteur revealed that microbes could cause many contagious diseases. His research led to improved public health, safer surgery, fewer deaths in war, and new ways to protect people and animals against disease.

Physics and chemistry had made great strides during the early part of the nineteenth century. As a result, many scientists of the time came to believe that all changes in matter were strictly physical or chemical. Pasteur, however, showed that some chemical reactions required the presence of living microorganisms. He also proved that microbes could not arise from nonliving matter. They had to come from other microbes. This, too, showed that living things had qualities that nonliving substances did not.

Pasteur broke down barriers between sciences, sharing insights among biology, chemistry, and medicine. He also founded new sciences. His research on crystals marked the beginning of stereochemistry, which studies the way atoms are arranged inside molecules. His studies of microorganisms helped to found the science of microbiology. His work on vaccination was the basis of immunology, the study of the way the body defends itself against disease.

Because Pasteur presented new ideas, other scientists and thinkers constantly argued with him. Even after his greatest successes, challengers made him prove his points all over again. Yet by the end of Pasteur's century, people almost worshiped him. Dignitaries from around the world attended the jubilee honoring his seventieth birthday. After Pasteur's death, one writer called him "the most perfect man who has ever entered the kingdom of Science."[4] Even today, if asked to name the person who symbolizes science at its finest, many people would choose Louis Pasteur.

Observation, Intuition, and Experiment

Pasteur was not the first person to come up with many of the ideas that made him famous, such as the belief that microorganisms could cause disease. Other scientists of the time also did important work that supported these ideas, yet none of these scientists became as well known. Why was Pasteur able to spread his ideas and change the thinking of his time so effectively?

One reason is Pasteur's devotion to work—he was one of the most productive scientists who ever lived. On the walls of the chapel where he is buried, carvings name nine areas of study to which he

Two of the nine mosaics that decorate the walls of the chapel where Pasteur is buried. Each carving represents an area of study to which Pasteur contributed.

contributed. Each area could have occupied most scientists for a lifetime. Pasteur's productivity reflected his endless capacity for work. Even after years of study and experiment had weakened his health, he said, "It would seem to me that I was committing a theft if I were to let one day go by without doing some work."[5] But work was not merely a duty. He once said, "Work . . . is the only thing which is entertaining."[6]

Long hours were only part of the story, however. Pasteur was successful because of the way he used his time. He followed the same pattern in each of his investigations. He began with a scientific question that intrigued him. This might have been a puzzling finding by another scientist or a practical problem that someone asked him to solve. Pasteur then read everything he could find about the subject. He also visited farms or factories to see the problem for himself.

René Dubos, an important Pasteur biographer, writes:

> He had the ability, and the discipline, to focus all his physical and mental energies on a given target. . . . One gets the impression that the intense "field" of interest which he created attracted within his range all the facts—large and small—pertinent to the solution of the problem which was preoccupying him.[7]

Pasteur's assistants described him staring at a sick sheep or a flask of microorganisms for hours. "Nothing escaped his nearsighted eye," said one co-worker, Emile Roux.[8] Pasteur carefully wrote down everything he observed, or that his assistants reported to him, in little notebooks.

After observation, the second step in Pasteur's investigations was intuition. Pasteur was rightly famous for his devotion to experiments and factual proof, but imagination played an equally large part in his genius. He seemed to know what his experiments would show, even before he carried them out. Pasteur was probably speaking of intuition when he said:

> The Greeks have given us one of the most beautiful words of our language, the word "enthusiasm"—[meaning] a God within. The grandeur of the acts of men is measured by the inspiration from which they spring. Happy is he who bears a God within![9]

Pasteur's power of concentration and attention to detail, combined with his intuition, help to explain what many have called his fantastic luck. When studying crystals, for example, he somehow chose one of the few groups of chemicals that

Pasteur was meticulous about testing all of his theories, discarding an idea if the results of experiments did not support it.

shows a clear relationship between the structure of their crystals and the structure of their molecules. Pasteur himself explained his so-called luck by saying, "Chance favors only the mind which is prepared."[10] Because he had prepared his mind, Pasteur noticed and used facts that other scientists missed. The result seemed like magic.

Pasteur tested all his ideas by painstaking experiment. As he told his co-workers and students, "Keep your . . . enthusiasm, . . . but let it ever be regulated by rigorous examinations and tests. Never advance anything which cannot be proved in a simple and decisive fashion."[11] If the results of his experiments did not support Pasteur's intuitive guesses, he discarded his ideas without a second thought. He could be persistent, however, if he believed that a line of thought had promise. Emile Roux recalled Pasteur's approach:

> How many times, in the presence of unforeseen difficulties, when we could not imagine how to get out of them, have I heard Pasteur tell us, "Let us do the same experiment over again; the essential is not to leave the subject."[12]

After experiments provided Pasteur with solid results, he used his imagination once more to make generalizations. These often went far beyond what his experiments had shown. For example, after doing studies on yeast, the microorganism involved in making wine and beer, he stated that some of the chemical processes that took place in yeast were probably found in all living things. His experiments had not given any evidence for this. Later research, however, showed the statement to be true. Basing a general theory on a small number of facts is a dangerous thing for a scientist to do, but the method almost always worked for Pasteur. Later research by other scientists supported most of his ideas.

Pasteur also had a strong effect during his era because he tried to make the public understand his work. Many educated people in the late nineteenth century were interested in science, and Pasteur took full advantage of this fact. He challenged scientists who disagreed with him to public demonstrations and contests. Some of these turned into social events that attracted the cream of Paris society.

In his public lectures, Pasteur proved his points with well-chosen words and simple, dramatic experiments. He often scolded and even made fun of his opponents. (He claimed, however, that his "lively and caustic manner" was used only "in the defense of truth.")[13] These features guaranteed a good show for his audience. They also helped newspaper reporters write vivid stories about his performances.

Besides giving talks to the general public, Pasteur took his discoveries directly to the people who needed them. He personally showed farmers how to protect their sheep and cattle from disease. He showed wine and beer makers how to produce drinks that would not spoil. In the evenings he answered endless letters from people who requested his advice or help.

A Man of Contradictions

Finally, Pasteur became a hero to many because they sensed the warmth that lay behind his sometimes harsh or cold appearance. It was true that he rarely spoke much, even to those closest to him. Emile Duclaux, another of Pasteur's co-workers, described the "Olympian [godlike] silence with which he loved to surround himself."[14] Pasteur's devoted wife, Marie, wrote to her children on her thirty-fifth anniversary, "Your father is absorbed in his thoughts, talks little, sleeps little, rises at dawn, and, in one word, continues the life I began

Pasteur's Importance to Medicine

In this excerpt from Microbes and Men, *Robert Reid, who has written biographies of several famous scientists, sums up Pasteur's importance to medicine.*

"At Pasteur's birthdate in 1822 life expectancy at birth was less than forty [years]. When he died, in 1895, that figure had been increased by many, many years and would continue to rise spectacularly; in another fifty years it would almost double. Much of that increase is directly attributable to the consistency of the work of Pasteur and of those who built on the foundations he laid. If greatness exists in science, Louis Pasteur was indisputably great."

Pasteur in his later years with his wife Marie and family. Pasteur's speeches and letters reveal a deep affection for his family.

with him this day thirty-five years ago."[15] Yet Pasteur's speeches and letters are filled with deep affection for his parents, sisters, wife, and children. He suffered greatly when three of his five children died in childhood. He always spoke admiringly of his teachers, even after his fame outgrew theirs. In turn, his family, friends, teachers, and pupils were devoted to him.

Strangers also remembered Pasteur's kindness. Farmers, silkworm breeders, and factory owners recalled the patience with which he answered their questions. When he visited his rabies vaccination clinic, he knew each patient's name. He tried especially hard to comfort the children. He always kept candies and small coins in a drawer for them.

Pasteur, then, was a man of contradictions. He was intuitive yet methodical, interested in general theories yet expert at solving practical problems. He was completely focused on his work, yet he could demonstrate both public showmanship and deep private affection. He expressed both halves of each contradiction with all the "faith and fire" of his passionate nature.[16] This many-sidedness, perhaps more than anything else, made Louis Pasteur both a great scientist and a great man.

1 The Tanner's Son

Louis Pasteur was born on December 27, 1822, in the village of Dôle, near the Jura Mountains in eastern France. His father, Jean Joseph Pasteur, was a tanner, a person who prepares animal skins to be made into leather. Pasteur men had been tanners for generations. Louis Pasteur's great-grandfather, for example, had worked as a

The house in the village of Dôle, France, where Louis Pasteur was born.

serf for the Count of Udressier. (A serf was a peasant required to stay on a lord's land, almost like a slave.) He bought his freedom for four pieces of gold in 1763 and then set up his own tanning business. Pasteur's grandfather was a tanner, too.

Young Louis helped his father with his work. The two soaked cattle hides in lime to soften them and loosen the hair on the skins. Then they rinsed and scraped the hides and covered them with dung from dogs or chickens. This part of the operation was called *puering*, from a French word meaning "to stink." Microbes in the dung digested material between the fibers of the hides. The Pasteurs then placed the hides in deep pits and mixed them with dried, ground-up oak bark. The bark contained a chemical called tannin. The tannin filled the gaps that the microbes had left between the skin fibers. It changed the hides into leather that was both supple and strong.

As a tanner, Louis Pasteur depended on microorganisms, those tiny living things that would become the focus of his life's work. The makers of beer, wine, bread, cheese, and many other common products depended on them as well. Yet at the time of Pasteur's childhood, few people, even among scientists, knew that microbes existed.

Pasteur Remembers His Parents

On July 14, 1883, the village of Dôle honored Pasteur by placing a memorial plaque on the house where he had been born. In accepting the honor, Pasteur shared memories of his parents. René Vallery-Radot, Pasteur's son-in-law, quotes Pasteur's speech in his biography, The Life of Pasteur.

"Oh! my father, my mother, dear departed ones, who lived so humbly in this little house, it is to you that I owe everything. Thy enthusiasm, my brave-hearted mother, thou has instilled it into me. If I have always associated the greatness of Science with the greatness of France, it is because I was impregnated with the feelings that thou hadst inspired. And thou, dearest father, whose life was as hard as thy hard trade, thou hast shown to me what patience and protracted [lengthy] effort can accomplish. It is to thee that I owe perseverance in daily work. Not only hadst thou the qualities which go to make a useful life, but also admiration for great men and great things. To look upwards, learn to the utmost, to seek to rise ever higher, such was thy teaching."

A Loving Family

Jean Joseph Pasteur had not spent all his life as a tanner. As a young man he was a sergeant in the army of Napoléon, the famous general who had made France the head of a great empire at the start of the nineteenth century. Napoléon himself awarded Pasteur the Ribbon of the Legion of Honor for bravery during fighting in Spain. Long after Napoléon was defeated by the British and fell from power, Jean Joseph Pasteur remembered his army days fondly. He wore his Legion of Honor medal when he went on Sunday walks after church. In the evenings he often relaxed by reading military histories of Napoléon's glory days. He taught his son to read with these same books. Louis Pasteur inherited from his father a powerful national pride that stayed with him all his life.

After Napoléon's empire collapsed in 1814, Jean Joseph Pasteur returned to his home in the village of Salins. People in the village began calling him "the old soldier." He was only twenty-five years old, but the sadness in his face made him seem older. Some of the sadness left him, however, when he met a lively young woman named Jeanne Roqui. Jean Joseph often saw her working in her family's garden, just across the river from his tannery. Her warmheartedness and enthusiasm balanced his more serious personality.

Jean Joseph and Jeanne married and moved to the nearby village of Dôle. Their marriage was a happy one, and in time they became the parents of a close and loving family which included Louis and three daughters. The Pasteurs moved twice more: first to Marnoz and then to the town of Arbois, where Louis Pasteur grew up with his three sisters, one older and two younger.

A Homesick Student

As a teenager, Louis Pasteur was fascinated with art. He even thought about becoming a professional artist. He drew detailed portraits of his parents and other people in Arbois. Albert Edelfeldt, a Finnish artist, saw some of these portraits in Pasteur's home in 1887 and described his impressions:

> They are extremely good and drawn with energy, full of character. . . . There is something of the great analyst in these portraits. . . . Had M. Pasteur selected art instead of science, France would count today one more able painter.[17]

Jean Joseph Pasteur, however, did not think much of art as a way to earn a living.

He hoped that Louis would become a teacher, perhaps even the headmaster of the Arbois school. Unfortunately, Louis seemed to show little academic promise. Most of his teachers rated him as only an average student. But Monsieur Romanet, the Arbois school's headmaster, guessed that some brilliance lay behind young Pasteur's slow, careful work. He encouraged Louis to prepare for the Ecole Normale Supérieure, the huge training college for teachers in Paris.

Pasteur knew he would need to take more classes before he could enter the Ecole Normale. When he was fifteen years old, he went to Paris to study. He attended a school run by a family named Barbet, with whom he also lived. He soon became so homesick, however, that he was physically ill. "If I could only get a whiff of the tannery yard," he told a friend, "I feel I should be cured."[18] Jean Joseph finally had to go to Paris and bring his son home.

Louis attended the Arbois school again for a short time. Then he took class-

These pastel portraits of Pasteur's parents, Jeanne and Jean Joseph, were painted by Pasteur when he was a teenager.

es at a larger "college" (really more like a high school) in Besançon, about thirty miles from Arbois. He began to study mathematics and physical science, doing well enough to give other students lessons in these subjects. He received bachelor's degrees in arts at Besançon in 1840 and in mathematics at Dijon in 1842.

Louis took the Ecole Normale Supérieure entrance examinations in 1842. He ranked fifteenth among twenty-two competitors. His score was good enough to get him into the school, but it did not meet his own standards. He returned to Paris to study again with the Barbets. Charles Chappuis, a good friend from Besançon, went with him.

Louis now took his studies more seriously. He wrote to his parents:

> I shall spend my Thursdays in a neighbouring library with Chappuis. . . . On Sundays we shall walk and work a little together; we hope to do some Philosophy on Sundays, perhaps too on Thursdays; I shall also read some literary works. Surely you must see that I am not homesick this time.[19]

Pasteur also attended public lectures at other schools. He was especially excited by the lectures of Jean-Baptiste Dumas, a famous chemist. Dumas spoke at the Sorbonne (the University of Paris). Louis described the atmosphere to his family:

> You cannot imagine what a crowd of people come to these lectures. The room is immense, and always quite full. We have to be there half an hour before the time to get a good place, as you would in a theatre; there is also a great deal of applause; there are always six or seven hundred people.[20]

Pasteur developed an interest in science as a student at the Ecole Normale.

Louis Pasteur took the entrance exam for the Ecole Normale again in 1843; this time he placed fourth. He entered the school that fall. He studied so hard that his family worried about his health. "You do work so immoderately," his father wrote. "Are you not injuring your eyesight by so much night work? Your ambition ought to be satisfied now that you have reached your present position!"[21]

But it was not. Inspired by Dumas, Pasteur decided that he wanted to learn chemistry. He introduced himself to Dumas and became the chemist's teaching assistant.

Though greatly interested in his studies with Dumas, Pasteur still intended to become a professor. "My chief desire is . . . to secure the opportunity to perfect myself in the art of teaching," he wrote.[22] But that desire was soon to change.

2 Right-Handed and Left-Handed Crystals

After classes at the Ecole Normale, Pasteur often walked through the streets of Paris with his friend Chappuis. The young men talked about what they had been studying. Chappuis discussed philosophy and literature. In his last year as a student, however, Pasteur had only one topic of conversation: Crystals, crystals, crystals.

Many scientists in the 1840s were intrigued by crystals. Crystals are solids with geometric shapes made up of flat sides or faces. In classes on crystallography, or the study of crystals, Pasteur learned that crystals of different chemical compounds have different shapes. Crystals of the mineral quartz, for example, have six sides. Crystals of table salt (sodium chloride) form cubes. Pasteur learned how to recognize different types of crystals. He used instruments to measure the angles between their faces and looked at small crystals under the microscope.

The Strange World of Crystals

Pasteur's teachers showed him that certain crystals could change light. One mineral

A magnified view of table salt crystals. Pasteur was intrigued by the effect of crystals on light.

Pasteur harbored a life-long interest in the study of crystals.

that forms such crystals is Iceland spar (calcium carbonate). If Pasteur looked at the sun through an Iceland spar crystal and turned it, he could see the sunlight dim and then brighten again. He was told that the crystal had polarized the light.

Scientists in Pasteur's time did not know why light changed after passing through crystals like those of Iceland spar. We now know that light is a kind of radiation and moves in waves. In ordinary white light, the waves travel in all directions. Polarized light is light in which polarizing crystals block all light waves except those that move in a single direction or plane. The light is said to be polarized along that plane. If you look at such light from the plane along which it is polarized, the light seems bright. If you look at the light from a different direction, it becomes dimmer or even disappears. This happens because most or all of the light waves are blocked and fail to reach your eyes. Sunglasses make bright sunlight seem dimmer because they are made of a material that polarizes light.

Jean-Baptiste Biot, a French chemist, had discovered around the beginning of the nineteenth century that certain quartz crystals could change the plane of polarized light. Some crystals turned the plane of the light to the right, while others turned the plane to the left. Researchers later found that such crystals had a unique face on either the right or the left that was unmatched by a similar face on the other side. Biot spoke of the crystals as right-handed and left-handed, like a pair of gloves. Right-handed and left-handed crystals were mirror images of each other. An English astronomer, John Herschel, suggested that the asymmetry of the crystals—their different right and left sides—caused them to bend polarized light.

Biot used these discoveries to learn about the basic structure of chemical compounds. He found that certain substances could change the plane of polarized light even when they were dissolved in liquid. In this solution form they contained no crystals. Biot guessed that the shape of the substances' molecules must somehow cause the change in polarized light. All the substances that affected polarized light while in solution were organic—that is, they were products of living things.

Pasteur became very interested in these organic solutions and their odd effect on light. He studied them with a newly invented device called a polarimeter. The polarimeter told him in which direction and to what degree each solution turned the plane of polarized light.

A Puzzling Report

Pasteur also pursued his crystal research in the school library. One day he read a re-

Jean-Baptiste Biot's research on crystals revealed that certain organic molecules could affect polarized light.

port that Biot had made to the Academy of Sciences in Paris in 1844. The report described some research done by Eilhard Mitscherlich, a famous chemist in Berlin. Mitscherlich had worked with two organic chemicals: tartaric acid and paratartaric acid. Tartaric acid occurred naturally in the tartar or crust that formed inside barrels when wine was made. In Pasteur's time, this chemical was purified in factories and then used in industrial processes such as dyeing and metal cleaning. Paratartaric acid was a much rarer and more mysterious substance. It had been found in a few tartaric acid factories starting around 1800. It was very similar to tartaric acid.

Mitscherlich said that a solution of a certain salt or compound of tartaric acid turned the plane of polarized light to the right. A solution of the same salt of paratartaric acid, however, had no effect on polarized light. And yet, Mitscherlich claimed, the two salts had exactly the same chemical formula: their molecules were made up of the same numbers and kinds of atoms. The crystals they formed as solids also appeared to be the same. Indeed, the two compounds seemed to be the same in every way except for their effect on polarized light.

Pasteur could not remove this seemingly obscure report from his mind. No matter what Mitscherlich said, Pasteur was sure some difference had to exist in the compounds that would explain their different effects on polarized light. He was determined to find that difference.

Pasteur passed his final examinations at the Ecole Normale in 1846. He ranked seventh in his class. He and thirteen other students then took a further exam to qualify them to teach physical sciences in secondary schools. Pasteur was rated third of

Tartaric acid built up naturally in the crust that formed inside barrels during the process of wine making. Pasteur was fascinated by the effect of the tartaric acid crystals on polarized light.

the four students who passed. "He will make an excellent professor," one examiner wrote.[23]

Students who graduated from the Ecole Normale had to teach for ten years, going wherever the Ministry of Public Instruction sent them. Pasteur, however, was now more interested in doing scientific research than in teaching. He persuaded Antoine Balard, a well-known chemist who taught at the Ecole Normale, to make him his laboratory assistant. That gained Pasteur extra time to study in Paris.

During this time, Pasteur started investigating the tartaric acid puzzle by making and studying nineteen different tartrates (salts of tartaric acid). He also finished two research papers, which earned him a doctor of science degree in August 1847. One paper concerned the effects of solutions on polarized light.

Events in the outside world briefly pulled Pasteur away from his crystals in 1848. In February the French people forced the country's ruler, Emperor Louis

Philippe, to quit the throne. For the second time in France's history, they made the country a republic, to be ruled by the people's elected representatives.

Pasteur wrote of the events to his parents:

> I am glad that I was in Paris during the February days. . . . A great and sublime doctrine . . . is now being unfolded before our eyes. . . . If it were necessary, I should heartily fight for the holy cause of the Republic.[24]

Neither the Second Republic nor Pasteur's enthusiasm lasted long, however. Four years later, France was once again an empire. The new emperor, Napoléon III, became Pasteur's patron and friend.

No mere change of government could keep Pasteur from his research for long. The revolution in Paris was less exciting than the revolution he was witnessing in his laboratory. Pasteur's polarimeter showed him that solutions of all the tartrates, like solutions of tartaric acid itself,

Demonstration for a Famous Chemist

Soon after Pasteur published his startling research on crystals, Jean-Baptiste Biot asked the young man to repeat the research in front of him. Pasteur was honored to meet the seventy-four-year-old Biot, whose research on crystals and solutions had inspired him. In a speech quoted in George Richardson's The Foundations of Stereo Chemistry, *Pasteur gives an account of the meeting.*

"He gave me some racemic [paratartaric] acid which he himself had previously examined and found to be entirely inactive toward polarized light. I prepared from it, in his presence, the sodium-ammonium double salt. . . . The solution was then placed in his laboratory and allowed slowly to evaporate; when 30 to 40 grams of the crystals had separated, he again called me to the College de France to collect and distinguish . . . the right and left rotating crystals from one another, under his direct observation. . . .

He prepared the carefully weighed solutions [of the right-handed and the left-handed crystals] and . . . called me again into his laboratory. He first put into the [polarimeter] . . . the one which should rotate toward the left. Without making a reading, but upon the instant, he noted a change of color in the two halves of the field of vision, he recognized an important laevorotation [left rotation].

Then the excited old man seized my hand and said: 'My dear child, I have all my life so loved this science that I can hear my heart beat for joy.'"

turned the plane of polarized light to the right. He believed that this happened because the molecules of these compounds were asymmetric, having right and left sides that were different. He expected the crystals of the substances to be asymmetric, too. Sure enough, when Pasteur looked under the microscope at crystals of the kind of tartrate Mitscherlich had used, he saw that (if all the crystals were lined up facing the same way) each crystal had one asymmetrical face. In other words, the crystals showed "handedness." Mitscherlich had not noticed this small irregularity.

Pasteur, however, spotted it at once because he was looking for it.

Pasteur next studied a sample of the matching paratartrate, or salt of paratartaric acid. In solution form, this compound did not affect the plane of polarized light, so Pasteur expected its crystals to be symmetrical. But when he looked at the crystals, he was amazed. "For an instant my heart stopped beating," he later declared, for all the crystals were asymmetrical.[25]

Many scientists would have been discouraged at seeing evidence that their theory might be wrong. Pasteur, however, just examined the uncooperative crystals more closely. He carefully lined them up along a single plane. Now he could see what had not been clear before. Half the crystals had an asymmetrical face on the left, while the other half had a similar face on the right. In other words, the paratartrate contained two kinds of crystals that were mirror images of each other. Pasteur concluded that the paratartrate did not change the plane of polarized light because the two forms canceled each other's effects.

A Great Discovery

Pasteur now set about proving his idea. He painstakingly separated the tiny crystals into two piles. All the left-handed crystals went into one pile and all the right-handed crystals into the other. He then made a solution of each pile and tested them in the polarimeter. Just as he had expected, the solution made from the left-handed crystals turned the plane of polarized light to the left. The solution from the right-handed crystals turned it to the right.

Pasteur was so excited that he dashed out of his laboratory. He threw his arms around the first man he saw, a laboratory assistant whom he hardly knew. "I have just made a great discovery!" he cried. "I am so happy that I am shaking all over and am unable to set my eyes again to the polarimeter!"[26] He dragged the startled young man off to the nearby Luxembourg Gardens and proceeded to tell him everything that had happened.

On May 22, 1848, Pasteur presented a paper to the French Academy of Sciences in Paris. The paper described his studies on tartaric and paratartaric acids. He concluded:

> I think that it is now plain that the property which certain molecules possess of deflecting [turning] the plane of polarization has as its immediate cause, or at least is closely connected with, the dissymmetry of those molecules.[27]

Pasteur's discovery confirmed and extended Biot's work. Pasteur showed that not only crystals but also molecules, the basic units of chemical compounds, could have asymmetric shapes. These shapes

A magnified view of tartaric acid crystals. Studying these crystals became a consuming passion for Pasteur.

could affect the physical behavior of the compounds, such as their effect on light.

Few young men of twenty-five years, with the ink hardly dry on their doctoral diplomas, were invited to present their work to the highly respected Academy of Sciences. Pasteur's pride and happiness were short-lived, however. That same month his mother suddenly died of a stroke. He stayed with his family for several weeks, too heartbroken to return to work.

The Minister's Daughter

In the fall of 1848 the Ministry of Public Instruction sent Pasteur to Dijon to teach secondary-school physics. However, Balard and other influential friends pressured the ministry to give him a better position. Within a few months, Pasteur was named professor of chemistry at the University of Strasbourg. He went to Strasbourg in January 1849 and moved in with an old friend, Pierre Bertin, who also taught there.

Bertin introduced Pasteur to important people at the university. One was Monsieur Laurent, the school's new minister. On a visit to the Laurent household Pasteur met one of the minister's daughters, twenty-two-year-old Marie. Blue-eyed Marie's cheerful, enthusiastic personality may have reminded Louis of the mother he had lost. At any rate, the careful and methodical Pasteur showed that he could make decisions quickly when he wanted to. Only two weeks after meeting Marie Laurent, he asked to marry her.

Following traditional custom, Pasteur made his request to Marie's father. But he wrote to Marie as well. "All that I beg of you, Mademoiselle [Miss], is that you will not judge me too hastily. . . . Time will show you that below my cold, shy and unpleasing exterior, there is a heart full of affection for you."[28]

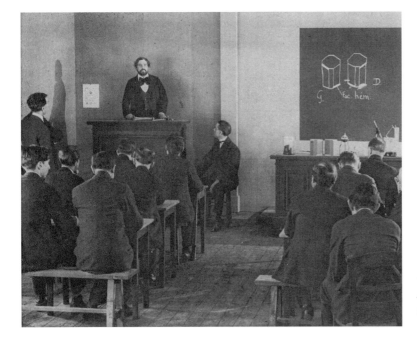

A 1923 still from a French film about Pasteur shows the great scientist teaching at the University of Strasbourg.

Marie and her father both agreed to Pasteur's proposal, and Marie and Louis were married on May 29, 1849. Their marriage like that of Pasteur's parents, proved a happy one. "Every quality I could wish for in a wife I find in her," Pasteur wrote to Chappuis.[29] Marie Pasteur, in turn, devoted her life to her husband and his work.

Once married, Pasteur quickly returned to his crystals. In 1850 he wrote to Chappuis:

> There are wonders hidden in crystallization, and, through it, the inmost construction of substances will one day be revealed. If you come to Strasbourg, you *shall* become a chemist; I shall talk to you of nothing but crystals.[30]

In 1851 the Pharmaceutical Society of Paris offered a prize to anyone who could answer two questions:

> 1. Do tartars exist that contain racemic acid [paratartaric acid] fully formed?
> 2. What are the conditions in which tartaric acid may be transformed into racemic acid?[31]

Since he had already worked with both substances, Pasteur decided to try to answer these questions.

To answer the first question, Pasteur visited tartaric acid factories in several parts of Europe in the fall of 1852. He concluded that the paratartaric acid was found mainly in the crudest tartars. Factories that started with partly refined tartars seldom produced paratartaric acid.

Pasteur then returned to Strasbourg and began work on the Pharmaceutical Society's second question. He finally succeeded in making paratartaric acid by heating cinchonine tartrate. Cinchonine came indirectly from the bark of a South American tree. This fact supported Pas-

Marie Laurent, a few years before her marriage to Pasteur.

teur's growing belief that all compounds with asymmetrical molecules came directly or indirectly from living things.

Pasteur presented his work to the Academy of Sciences in August 1853. The Pharmaceutical Society awarded him its fifteen-hundred-franc prize. He used half the money to buy better equipment for his laboratory. The French government also awarded the young chemist the Red Ribbon of the Legion of Honor, because his research was useful to French industries that used tartaric acid. Pasteur's father had won this same award for a different kind of service to his country.

Birth of a New Science

Late in his life, Pasteur would say that his early work with crystals was his favorite research project of all. This work was also important. It became the foundation of a new scientific field called stereochemistry. This science studies the way atoms are arranged in space to form molecules.

In the mid-1870s, stereochemists showed that atoms of the element carbon form bonds that lead to production of asymmetric molecules. All organic compounds contain carbon. The discovery about carbon bonds thus supported Pasteur's prediction that organic molecules would be asymmetric. Stereochemists later found that many carbon-containing molecules have two or more forms that contain the same number and kind of atoms, but have geometric differences. These forms often have different qualities or properties.

Stereochemists found that asymmetric molecules with different "handedness" could have different effects on living things. Pasteur himself saw an example of this in 1857. He discovered that certain microorganisms could use the right-handed but not the left-handed form of one tartrate as food. "Bodies [substances] may be entirely changed in character by a re-arrangement of the atoms in the chemical molecule," he said.[32] Although some of Pasteur's beliefs about the relationship between the structure of molecules and their effects on polarized light and other properties eventually proved to be wrong, his basic ideas were correct.

An Asymmetrical Universe

Pasteur's belief that all asymmetrical molecules came from living things played an important role in shaping his future research. When he tried to explain this idea, he grew

Louis and Marie Pasteur in a formal portrait. Louis wrote that he had "a heart full of affection" for Marie.

almost mystical. "The universe is a dissymmetrical whole. I am inclined to think that life . . . must be a function of the dissymmetry of the universe and of the consequences it produces."[33] The planet Earth itself, Pasteur pointed out, could be said to be asymmetrical because it moves. It is not the same as its mirror image, because the mirror image would turn in the opposite direction. Pasteur thought that asymmetric forces in nature might cause the chemicals in living things to be asymmetric. As he wondered about the relationship between asymmetry and life, his attention began to turn from his tidy crystals to the less clear-cut world of living things.

3 Bubbling and Brewing

In 1854 Pasteur became professor of chemistry and dean of the science faculty at the University of Lille. He moved to this northern French city with his growing family, which now included daughters Jeanne (born 1850) and Cécile (born 1853) and a son, Jean-Baptiste (born 1851). The Pasteurs would eventually have two more daughters, Marie-Louise in 1858 and Camille in 1863.

A Practical Scientist

Pasteur's work in Lille changed his approach to science. Until then he had been a "pure" scientist, investigating questions because they interested him or because they might reveal something about the world of nature. But Lille was an industrial city. Its leaders wanted the head of their newly reorganized science faculty to relate his research and teaching to practical concerns.

Pasteur obliged. He taught chemistry by describing its role in the region's industrial processes. He took his students to visit factories in Lille, in other French cities, and even in the nearby country of Belgium. In *Louis Pasteur: Free Lance of Science* René Dubos writes:

Within two years after his arrival at Lille, the scientific philosopher had been converted into a servant of society; and from that time on, most of his efforts were to be oriented, directly or indirectly, by the desire to solve the practical problems of his environment.[34]

In the fall of 1856, a Lille factory owner named Bigo asked Pasteur to help him

A portrait of Pasteur at age thirty. Two years later he would become the head of the science faculty at the University of Lille.

with a problem. Bigo's factory made alcohol from beet sugar. This kind of alcohol was used in industry, not for drinking. All summer, Bigo and Lille's other alcohol makers had been finding that most of their product was spoiled. Bigo hoped Pasteur could find out why and tell him how to prevent the spoilage.

Pasteur set out to learn about alcohol making. He visited Lille's alcohol-making plants. Sometimes helped by Bigo's son, he made experiments both in his laboratory and in the factories. As Marie Pasteur wrote to Pasteur's father, "Louis . . . is now up to his neck in beet juice. He spends all his days in the distillery."[35]

Conflicting Theories of Fermentation

Alcohol is made from sugar through a process called fermentation. In the case of wine, the sugar comes from grapes. In beer, it comes from barley and hops.

When sugar-containing plant matter is left alone for several weeks, the material begins to bubble as if it were boiling. The word *ferment* means 'boil'.

People all over the world have used fermentation from ancient times. Fermentation helps to make bread, cheese, and vinegar as well as alcoholic drinks. Pasteur's father relied on a type of fermentation when he spread dung on his hides to prepare them for tanning. All fermentation processes break down organic matter that contains sugar or starch.

In the late 1700s, the French chemist Lavoisier showed that alcoholic fermentation changed sugar into alcohol and carbon dioxide. The carbon dioxide bubbled out as a gas. Oxygen seemed necessary for the process. Beyond this, scientists could not agree on how fermentation took place.

The most popular theory said that fermentation was strictly a chemical reaction. This was the view of Justus von Liebig of Munich, one of Europe's leading chemists at the time Pasteur began to study the problem. Liebig said that fermentation occurred

A bubbling vat of fermenting white wine. Pasteur and other scientists of the nineteenth century disagreed about what caused fermentation.

Practical Science

"Where in your families will you find a young man whose curiosity and interest will not immediately be awakened when you put into his hands a potato, when with that potato he may produce sugar, with that sugar alcohol, and with that alcohol ether and vinegar? Where is he that will not be happy to tell his family in the evening that he has just been working out an electric telegraph? . . . Such studies are seldom if ever forgotten. It is somewhat as if geography were to be taught by travelling; such geography is remembered because one has seen the places. In the same way your sons will not forget what the air we breathe contains when they have once analysed it, when in their hands and under their eyes the admirable properties of its elements have been resolved."

because of "molecular movement." By means of this movement, matter that was breaking down caused nearby matter to do the same. No living things were needed for the process. Liebig thought all decay of organic matter took place in this way.

Liebig's ideas fit the mid-nineteenth-century emphasis on physics and chemistry. These "hard sciences" seemed more precise than biology, the study of living things. Many scientists tried to treat living things as if they were the same as nonliving matter.

Not all scientists agreed with Liebig, however. In the 1670s Antonie van Leeuwenhoek, a Dutchman, had seen small, round bodies in yeast when he looked at it under a microscope. Yeast was a material that brewers added to barley to make beer. In 1835 the French scientist Cagniard-Latour claimed that these yeast bodies were living things. Using the improved microscopes of his time, he watched the bodies grow and reproduce. He and several other scientists thought these yeast bodies played some role in fermentation.

Liebig agreed that they might, but he insisted that they played that role only after they died. He wrote:

> This yeast does not embarrass me; it enters my [idea] system. If you admit that it lives you also admit that it dies. Then it is in dying that it acts, as a consequence of the decomposition [decay] that it undergoes at this time.[36]

In other words, yeast was just another source of organic material to be broken down.

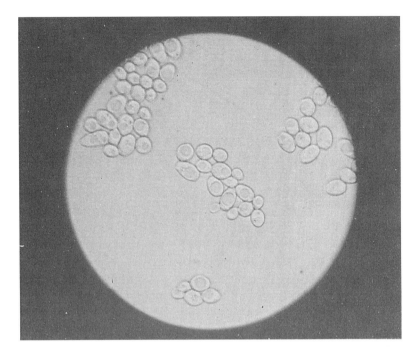

A view of a yeast culture under a microscope. Pasteur studied these round bodies to determine their role in alcohol production.

Pasteur suspected from the beginning that the yeast supporters were right. In 1855 he had discovered that one kind of alcohol had two forms. Both forms had the same chemical composition, but the atoms were arranged differently in their molecules. One form changed the plane of polarized light. According to Pasteur's study of crystals, this meant that the molecules of that form must be asymmetrical. Pasteur believed that only substances made by living things could have asymmetrical molecules. He therefore guessed that living things must carry out the fermentation that made alcohol. He wanted to study alcoholic fermentation not only to help the Lille alcohol makers, but also to learn more about the relationship between molecular asymmetry and the chemistry of life.

When Pasteur looked at Monsieur Bigo's fermenting beet juice through a microscope, he saw the same round bodies that Cagniard-Latour and others had described in yeast. He also found a way to tell when a batch of juice was starting to spoil. As Bigo's son reported:

> Pasteur . . . noticed . . . that the [yeast] globules were round when fermentation was healthy, that they lengthened when alteration began, and were quite long when fermentation became lactic [produced lactic acid, a sour substance]. This very simple method allowed us to watch the process and to avoid the failures in fermentation which we used so often to meet with.[37]

Lactic Acid Fermentation

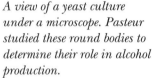

Besides studying alcoholic fermentation, Pasteur began to investigate the kind of fermentation that made lactic acid. Such fermentation meant disaster in Bigo's vats, but it was useful in making butter and cheese. In fact, the acid received its name because it was most often found in sour milk. (*Lactic* comes from a Latin word meaning 'milk'.) Lactic fermentation breaks down a molecule of sugar into two molecules of lactic acid.

Looking back on Pasteur's career, Louis Pasteur Vallery-Radot, Pasteur's grandson, thought Pasteur chose to study lactic fermentation because he suspected he could use it to prove Liebig wrong. Liebig admitted that yeast played some role in alcoholic fermentation and that it might be a living thing. His main reason for saying that yeast could not *cause* fermentation was that no microorganisms had been found in other kinds of fermentation, including lactic fermentation. If Pasteur could show that a microbe caused lactic fermentation, he would go far toward proving that microbes also caused other kinds of fermentation, including the kind that made alcohol.

When Pasteur looked at souring milk, he saw blotches of gray matter on top of the fermenting material. Under the microscope, the gray matter proved to contain round bodies much smaller than those in yeast. These bodies were always present when lactic fermentation took place, and they grew in number as the fermentation went on. Pasteur saw the same bodies in soured batches of beet juice. He believed that they were alive and that they caused lactic fermentation. He thought they were another kind of yeast. (They actually belong to the group of microorganisms called bacteria.) No one had spotted these creatures before because they were hard to tell from curdled protein and other matter in the milk. As with the tartaric

acid crystals, Pasteur saw something other scientists had missed because he was looking for it.

Pasteur next made a mixture of sugar, chalk (calcium carbonate), and yeast water. Yeast water was the liquid left after brewer's yeast had been boiled and filtered. This liquid contained no whole yeast cells, living or dead. Pasteur added it to provide the nitrogen-containing (protein) matter that he expected the lactic yeast to need as food. He then added a tiny amount of the gray matter from lactic fermentation.

A day later the mixture showed clear signs of fermentation. The liquid had turned cloudy, and bubbles of carbon dioxide gas rose from it. After a while Pasteur recovered calcium lactate from the

Pasteur saw microorganisms like these when he looked at soured milk under a microscope.

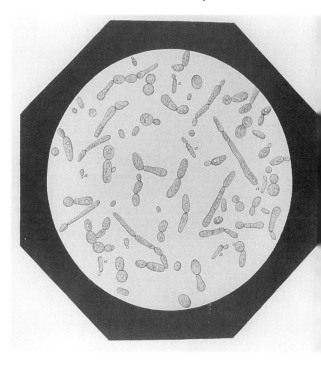

Little Animals

A Dutchman named Antonie van Leeuwenhoek was the first person to see microorganisms under a microscope. In 1676 he wrote this description of a "little animal" he found in rainwater. Leeuwenhoek's account appears in Samuel Rapport and Helen Wright's Great Adventures in Medicine.

"The first sort [of creature] I several times observed to consist of five, six, seven, or eight clear globules without being able to discern any film that held them together. . . . When these animalcula [little animals] or living atoms moved, they put forth two little horns, continually moving. The space between these two horns was flat, though the rest of the body was roundish, sharpening a little toward the end, where they had a tail, near four times the length of the whole body, of the thickness, by my microscope, of a spider's web; at the end of which appeared a globule of the size of one of those which made up the body. These little creatures, if they chanced to light on the least filament or string, or other particle, were entangled therein, extending their body in a long round and endeavoring to disentangle their tail. Their motion of extension and contraction continued awhile; and I have seen several thousands of these poor little creatures, within the space of a grain of . . . sand, lie fast clustered together in a few filaments."

---

mixture. This compound had been made from the chalk and lactic acid. Its existence proved that lactic acid had been formed.

This experiment supported the idea that the microbes in the gray matter caused lactic fermentation. It also showed that lactic fermentation was much like the fermentation that made alcohol. It started with the same substances, but it resulted in different products because a different kind of microorganism carried it out.

In his lactic acid experiments, Pasteur set up a technique that became a basic part of microbiology. First he isolated a certain kind of microorganism, or separated it from other kinds. Then he let it multiply in a nutrient solution or medium. (The resulting group of the microorganisms, all of one kind, is called a culture.) Finally, he showed that the reaction that the microbe was suspected of causing occurred in the medium.

Pasteur and others later modified this technique to identify microorganisms that caused disease. Instead of looking for a chemical reaction in a culture, they injected the culture into animals. Then they waited to see whether the animals came down with the disease that the microbes in the culture were suspected of causing.

In another part of his lactic acid experiments, Pasteur exposed his nutrient

Lactic acid, most often found in sour milk, came from a fermentation process that was useful in making butter and cheese. However, the same kind of fermentation resulted in a spoiled product for the alcohol industry. Pasteur experimented unceasingly to determine how lactic acid was made.

medium to the air without adding any matter from lactic fermentation. Several kinds of microorganisms grew in the mixture. Pasteur wrote:

> What takes place in fermentations may be compared to what occurs in a plot of land that is not seeded. It soon becomes crowded with various plants and insects that are mutually harmful.
>
> One of the essential conditions for good fermentations is the purity of the ferment . . . [and] its free develop-

ment . . . with the help of a nutrient well adapted to its individual nature.[38]

Pasteur discovered that different kinds of microorganisms required different nutrient chemicals in their medium, just as different animals need different foods. This finding suggested a technique for separating kinds of microorganisms. It also offered a way to help Bigo and others who wanted to produce only certain kinds of fermentations. They could produce more of a certain kind of microbe by providing a medium with the nutrients that particular microbe needed most.

Pasteur presented his "Memoir on Lactic Fermentation" to the Society of Sciences in Lille in August 1857. Later the same year he published a paper declaring that yeast caused alcoholic fermentation. His conclusions in these papers, like those in his studies on crystals, reached well beyond the specific results of his experiments. The paper showed that microorganisms caused important changes in organic matter. Biographer René Dubos calls Pasteur's lactic fermentation paper "the Manifesto [public declaration] of the germ theory."[39]

Fermentation Requires Living Things

Pasteur's lactic fermentation paper was his last work at Lille. That fall the Ecole Normale Supérieure asked him to join its faculty, and he gladly accepted. He looked forward to returning to his old school and the exciting scientific life of Paris.

Pasteur became the assistant director of scientific studies and general administration at the Ecole Normale. Besides planning science courses, he supervised student housing, food, medical care, and discipline. He kept this administrative position until 1867. His laboratory remained at the Ecole Normale long after that.

A chief science professor at most colleges today would have a shiny, well-equipped laboratory. No such arrangement awaited Pasteur. He had to set up his laboratory in two hot, little rooms in the school's attic. He bought or made all his own equipment. In 1859 he obtained a somewhat larger work area and his first

laboratory assistant. His laboratory space was still limited, however. For example, the warming closet or incubator in which he kept his cultures of microorganisms was under a staircase. He had to crawl on his hands and knees to reach it.

Tragedy marred Pasteur's pleasure at returning to Paris. In September 1859 his oldest daughter, Jeanne, died of typhoid fever. This contagious disease is caused by microorganisms. Jeanne was only nine years old. At the end of the year Pasteur wrote to his father, "I cannot keep my thoughts from my poor little girl, so good, so happy in her little life, whom this fatal year now ending has taken away from us."[40]

Pasteur eased his grief by burying himself in work—a reaction he was to repeat when later tragedies struck. He knew he had not yet completely proved his case against Liebig. Liebig insisted that nonliving organic matter caused fermentation, and Pasteur's yeast water contained such matter. In order to show once and for all that Liebig was wrong, Pasteur would have to produce fermentation without any organic matter except microorganisms.

After many trials, he found a way to do this. In 1860 he announced that he had grown yeast and produced alcoholic fermentation in a solution containing only sugar, water, ammonium salts (which provided the nitrogen that the yeasts normally got from organic matter), and a few other mineral compounds. Once again Pasteur concluded, "Fermentation is a process correlative with life."[41] In other words, fermentation is always associated with living things.

Pasteur's co-worker and biographer, Emile Duclaux, said that this paper's attack on the theories of Liebig was "a series

Pasteur spent endless hours in his laboratory to prove that fermentation requires living things.

of blows straight from the shoulder, delivered with agility and assurance."[42] Liebig did not give up, but more and more other scientists decided that Pasteur was right.

Later research showed that Pasteur and Liebig were both partly right. Pasteur was correct in saying that microorganisms always cause fermentation in nature. Liebig, however, was also correct in maintaining that fermentation is a chemical reaction and can be made to occur without living things. In 1897 two German scientists, Eduard and Hans Buchner, showed that a substance extracted from yeast could cause fermentation without any living yeast being present. They called their extract zymase.

Zymase is one of a large group of organic compounds called enzymes. All en-

zymes came originally from living things, though many can now be made artificially in the laboratory. The cells of plants and animals use many of the same enzymes that mircroorganisms do. Enzymes act as catalysts; that is, they speed up chemical reactions without taking part in them. They affect reactions involved in fermentation, digestion, putrefaction, and other processes in which organic matter is changed.

The modern science of biochemistry studies these and other chemical reactions that take place in living things. By showing that microorganisms carried out chemical reactions, Pasteur in effect put the "bio" in biochemistry. His next research would explore even more deeply the relationship between living and nonliving matter.

Chapter

4 Where Do Germs Come From?

In studying fermentation, Pasteur felt he was exploring "the impenetrable mystery of Life and Death."[43] He had shown that living microorganisms were required for this process, which Liebig and others had thought could take place in nonliving matter. The next question to be answered, Pasteur thought, was where these microorganisms came from. Many scientists of his time believed that microbes were made from decaying organic substances. If living things could be formed from nonliving material, the difference between living and nonliving matter would not be great. If, on the other hand, living things could arise only from living parents, Pasteur's belief in the unique qualities of living matter would be confirmed.

Animals Out of Nothing?

The process by which living things were thought to arise from nonliving matter was called spontaneous generation. Belief in spontaneous generation had a long history. The ancient Greek philosopher Aristotle, for example, had maintained that frogs and salamanders came from slime. Van Helmont, a seventeenth-century scientist, claimed he could breed mice by leaving a dirty shirt in a bin containing wheat or cheese. Most people were sure that flies and certain other insects were formed spontaneously in rotting meat.

Around 1675 (at the same time Leeuwenhoek was discovering microorganisms) an Italian named Francisco Redi proved that flies and their wormlike young, called maggots, were not generated spontaneously. Redi wrapped meat in

Seventeenth-century scientist Francisco Redi disproved the then common belief that flies and maggots arise from dead matter.

thin cloth. He showed that maggots appeared outside the cloth but not inside it. He watched flies lay eggs on the cloth and saw the eggs hatch into maggots. Earlier observers had not noticed these eggs because the eggs were very small.

By the end of the seventeenth century, experiments like Redi's had convinced most people that creatures big enough to see with the naked eye did not arise from dead matter. Scientists were still unsure about microscopic life, however. They thought microbes might be created from decaying matter by a mysterious "vegetative force." Scientists in Pasteur's time were very interested in the question of spontaneous generation. If this question could be answered, they felt, much would be revealed about the origin and nature of life.

Microbes in Dust

Pasteur was already thinking about spontaneous generation when he read a short paper published in December 1858. Félix Pouchet, director of the Rouen Museum of Natural History, was the author. In the paper, Pouchet claimed to have conducted an experiment that proved spontaneous generation could occur. Pouchet heated a flask of water to kill any microbes that might be in it. He then put into it a hay mixture that had also been heated. He did this in a way that, he thought, prevented any new microbes from entering. Yet microorganisms grew in the mixture after a few days. Pouchet claimed, therefore, that the microbes that grew in the hay had to have been generated spontaneously.

Pasteur wrote to Pouchet on February 28, 1859. He stated that he was not sure whether spontaneous generation could occur. He believed, however, that errors in Pouchet's experiment had allowed dust from the air to carry microbes into the flask. Pouchet therefore had not really proved that spontaneous generation could take place.

To prove that microbes existed in dust, Pasteur put nutrient-containing broth in flasks. He then melted the flasks' necks in a flame and drew them out into narrow, open, S-shaped tubes with a bend at the bottom. Because of their shape these became known as "swan-neck" flasks. Pasteur boiled the liquid in the flasks and let them sit in still air. Months later, no germs had grown in the flasks, even though air could get into them. Pasteur said this was because all the germ-laden dust had been trapped in the bend of the flasks' necks. To prove this, he tipped some of the flasks so that a little broth poured into the bend in the flasks' necks. Microorganisms began to grow in the broth within a few days. The same thing happened if he broke off a flask's neck so dusty air could enter.

Air in Different Places

If microorganisms were generated spontaneously, Pasteur reasoned, they would grow anywhere. If they were carried by dust in the air, however, they would be more likely to appear in some locations than in others. In 1860 he carried out a series of experiments that compared samples of air from different places.

All these experiments used flasks that tapered to a small opening on top. Pasteur put nutrient broth into the flasks, boiled it, and sealed the flasks' necks shut. He

"Life Is a Germ and a Germ Is Life"

In 1864 Pasteur showed an audience the flasks he had prepared years before. The broth in the flasks was still free of microbes, even though air could enter the flasks, because the shape of the necks kept dust out. In his biography of Pasteur, René Vallery-Radot quotes Pasteur.

"And, therefore, gentlemen, I could point to that liquid and say to you, I have taken my drop of water from the immensity of creation, and I have taken it full of the elements appropriated to the development of inferior beings. And I wait, I watch, I question it!—begging it to recommence [begin again] for me the beautiful spectacle of the first creation. But it is dumb [silent], dumb since these experiments were begun several years ago; it is dumb because I have kept it from the only thing man does not know how to produce: from the germs which float in the air, from Life, for Life is a germ and a germ is Life. Never will the doctrine of spontaneous generation recover from the mortal blow of this simple experiment."

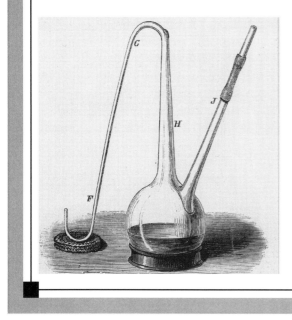

The swan-neck flask used by Pasteur to prove that microbes exist in dust.

carried the flasks to the places he wished to test. Then he broke open the neck of each flask. He did this while holding the flask above his head so that dust on his clothes would not get into it. Air, along with any dust and germs it might be carrying, rushed into the flask. Pasteur then quickly sealed the flask shut once more with the flame of a portable lamp. By opening groups of flasks in different places and counting how many showed growth of microorganisms, Pasteur could see how microbes in the air were distributed.

Pasteur performed most of his 1860 experiments during his summer vacation

Carrying a case of flasks, Pasteur climbed high into the Alps to test the mountain air.

(August and September). As usual, he spent this vacation with his father in Arbois. That summer Pasteur opened twenty flasks on the road to Dôle, some distance from the nearest houses. Microorganisms grew in eight of them. He opened twenty more on Mount Poupet in the nearby Jura range, and only five showed growth. Accompanied by a mule carrying his case of flasks, he next climbed two thousand meters into the Alps. Only one of the flasks he opened there became infected. "Where the air is pure and relatively free from floating matter it rarely gives rise to living forms," Pasteur concluded.[44] He found the most microorganisms in air near where human beings pursued activities such as farming.

Pouchet and two of his supporters decided to beat Pasteur at his own game. In the summer of 1860 and again in 1863, they too went on expeditions. They followed a procedure similar to Pasteur's, but germs grew in nearly all of their flasks. "Therefore, . . ." they said, "the production of a new being devoid of [lacking] parents, but formed at the expense of . . . organic matter, is for us a reality."[45]

The Debate Continues

Pasteur claimed that the difference in results occurred because his opponents had not carried out their experiments carefully enough. The difference was actually caused by something that was not recognized for another fifteen years. Pasteur used yeast water as his medium, but Pouchet used hay in water. Both men assumed that all microorganisms could be killed by boiling. A common microbe that lives on hay, however, can form resistant bodies called spores. These survive even lengthy boiling. Pasteur's sealed flasks were free of living microorganisms, but Pouchet's were not. The microbes in the hay began growing as soon as fresh air entered Pouchet's flasks, whether the air contained other germs or not.

The argument between Pasteur and Pouchet attracted wide attention. Many educated people of Pasteur's time, not just scientists, were interested in the question of spontaneous generation. Newspapers wrote stories about it. People went to hear lectures on it. For example, the elite of Paris society, including one member of the royal family, attended a lecture about spontaneous generation that Pasteur gave at the Sorbonne on April 7, 1864.

The debate about spontaneous generation was often tied to the equally passionate debate that raged over Charles Darwin's *Origin of Species*, published in 1859. According to René Dubos, "For many complex reasons, the problem of origins—of life and of species—was the order of the day, and a very sensitive point of nineteenth-century consciousness."[46] By disagreeing with scientists who believed in spontaneous generation, Pasteur made himself a part of both debates.

Public reaction to Darwin and Pasteur was closely tied to religion. Opponents of Darwin's theory of evolution claimed that it contradicted the account of creation in the Bible's Book of Genesis. Many people said that the theory of spontaneous generation also went against the Bible because the theory said that creation of life was still going on. Other groups called the Bible supporters unscientific. Because Pasteur spoke against spontaneous generation, these groups claimed he was defending traditional religious views. Pasteur was a Catholic, but he denied that his religion had anything to do with his stand on the controversy:

There is here no question of religion, philosophy, atheism [belief that God

An illustration from Pasteur's 1861 article refuting the theory of spontaneous generation. The drawings are illustrations of experiments he performed to prove that airborne bacteria cause decay.

does not exist], materialism, or spiritualism. . . . They do not matter to me as a scientist. It is a question of fact; when I took it up I was as ready to be convinced by experiments that spontaneous generation exists as I am now persuaded that those who believe it are blindfolded.[47]

The Academy of Sciences tried to settle the spontaneous generation question in 1864. They asked Pasteur and Pouchet to repeat some of their experiments before a committee of scientists. When the committee met on June 22, Pasteur showed several flasks he had filled with air in the Alps in the summer of 1860. The liquid in the flasks was as clear and empty of microorganisms as it had been when he sealed them. Pasteur opened one flask to show that it contained normal air and that microorganisms could grow in it.

Pouchet and his friends did not perform any experiments for the committee. They therefore lost the contest by default. Ironically, as several of Pasteur's biographers have pointed out, Pouchet probably would have won if he had presented his experiments. Because spores of hay bacteria were already in his flasks, the flasks would have shown growth of microbes under any conditions.

The Persistent Question

The debate on spontaneous generation continued for over ten years. In 1877 the English physicist John Tyndall provided evidence against the theory that was even more convincing than Pasteur's. Tyndall also discovered the heat-resistant spores of the hay bacteria and certain other microorganisms.

Pasteur returned to the spontaneous generation question in the 1870s as well. His opponent this time was an English doctor, Henry Bastian. While trying to disprove Bastian's claims, Pasteur learned that some of his own methods of heating to kill microorganisms were not completely effective. He modified them. Similarly, Tyndall worked out a way of heating that killed spores.

Pasteur never claimed to prove that spontaneous generation was impossible. As he himself said in 1878, "Spontaneous generation? I have been looking for it for twenty years, but I have not yet found it, although I do not think that it is an impossibility."[48] Scientists still do not know how the first living things arose on earth. They do not know whether humans will someday create chemicals or machines that can reproduce themselves like living things. Pasteur and Tyndall did show, however, that spontaneous generation does not happen under ordinary conditions.

While trying to settle the question of spontaneous generation, Pasteur and his supporters discovered a great deal about where and under what conditions microorganisms can live. They also learned several ways to kill harmful microbes. These discoveries were important additions to the young science of microbiology. Later, after microbes were shown to cause disease, the findings were useful to medicine as well. They helped doctors figure out how disease microbes spread and how such microbes could be stopped.

5 Savior of French Industry

An important factor in Louis Pasteur's productivity was his ability to work on several scientific projects at once. At the same time he was trying to disprove the theory of spontaneous generation, he continued his experiments on fermentation. These experiments brought him growing fame.

Representatives of several fermentation-related industries came to Pasteur during the early 1860s. As Monsieur Bigo had done in Lille, they asked him to solve problems that were costing them money. Thus, while Pasteur was exploring the theoretical question of the origin of life, he was also dealing with practical puzzles such as what made wine spoil and how to make better vinegar. Both theoretical and

practical research deepened his understanding of microorganisms.

Pasteur made one major discovery by examining spoiled butter. Such butter smelled bad because it contained a substance called butyric acid. Butyric acid was made from lactic acid by fermentation. Pasteur found that very active, rod-shaped bacteria seemed to cause this fermentation.

Pasteur was amazed by the way these bacteria behaved after they had been on a microscope slide a short time. As the drop of liquid around them slowly dried up, the germs in the middle of the drop remained active. Those near the edges, however, became still and seemed to die. The other microorganisms he had studied would

A woman pours milk into a barrel to make butter. Those in the butter industry were grateful when Pasteur discovered the bacteria that causes butter to spoil.

crowd near the edges of the drop, where oxygen was abundant. Furthermore, when Pasteur bubbled air through a solution in which butyric fermentation was occurring, the fermentation stopped. He concluded that these new microorganisms could live without oxygen. "In fact," he wrote in a report to the Academy of Sciences in February 1861, "air kills them. . . . This is, I think, the first known instance . . . of an animal capable of living without free oxygen."[49] Before this, scientists had thought that no living thing could survive without oxygen gas from the air. Pasteur had discovered a form of life that differed from others in a major way.

Pasteur later found other microbes that could live without oxygen gas. He called them *anaerobic*, which means "without air." (He called microorganisms that required air *aerobic*.) He showed that certain kinds of anaerobic microbes cause putrefaction or decay. Putrefaction is the process by which microbes break down animal matter. It is similar to fermentation, which breaks down plant matter. He also learned that some microbes can live either with or without oxygen gas. The yeast that causes alcoholic fermentation is one of these. Fermentation lets microbes obtain oxygen from organic matter instead of the air.

Even more important, Pasteur theorized that the cells of plants and animals carried out the same chemical processes as microorganisms. "Fermentation should be possible in all types of cells," he wrote. "All living beings are ferments [capable of causing fermentation] under certain conditions of their life."[50] René Dubos calls Pasteur's connection of the chemical processes in microbes with those in other living cells "perhaps the most original and profound thought of his long career."[51] In this inspired guess, Pasteur showed a way in which all living things were alike. Later research confirmed his idea.

Research on Vinegar

Pasteur had made his studies of spoiled butter mainly to satisfy his own curiosity. His next scientific project, however, was done to solve an industrial problem. Vinegar making was a major industry in the French city of Orléans. Like the alcohol makers of Lille four years before, the vinegar makers of Orléans were having trouble producing a dependable product. They asked Pasteur to help them.

Vinegar is sour because it contains acetic acid. This acid is made from alcohol by fermentation. When vinegar was being made from wine, a sort of slime formed on the surface of the liquid. Vinegar manufacturers called this unpleasant-looking material "mother of vinegar." They knew it was necessary for vinegar making, but they did not know why. Pasteur found a fungus (a multicelled, plantlike microorganism) in the "mother of vinegar." He showed that this fungus could make acetic acid.

Pasteur published the results of his research on acetic acid fermentation in July 1861. A year later he presented to the Academy of Sciences an improved industrial process for making vinegar. He patented this process to keep others from doing so. Then, however, he allowed the patent to become public property.

Older ways of making vinegar had been based only on guesswork. Pasteur's method, however, grew out of his knowledge of the microorganisms that made vinegar. His process made vinegar making easier to control. It saved vinegar manufacturers millions of francs.

Diseases of Wine

Scientists as well as industrialists admired Pasteur's fermentation research. Because of this growing respect, Pasteur was elected to the Academy of Sciences, France's top scientific organization, in December 1862. The academy had just sixty members, and a new member could be added only when an old one died. Half the members had to vote yes before a candidate was accepted.

Pasteur was presented to Emperor Napoléon III in March 1863. In July of that year, the emperor asked him to solve another expensive industrial problem. At the time, 2 million hectares of French land were used to grow wine grapes. France produced over 5 million francs' worth of wine each year, and French wines were in demand all over the world. Unfortunately, they often spoiled before they reached their destinations. Different kinds of wine went bad in different ways. The emperor hoped that Pasteur could find causes and cures for these "wine diseases."

Pasteur began his wine research in the summer of 1863, while his opponents in the spontaneous generation controversy were busy climbing the Alps. He continued his studies in the summer of 1864. He and a new assistant, Emile Duclaux, set up a laboratory in an empty café in Arbois. They got the local carpenter and blacksmith to make some of their equipment. Pasteur then asked his Arbois friends to bring him samples of sick and healthy wines. He visited nearby wine cellars to gather other samples.

Pasteur studied each sample under the microscope. He found that wine diseases were caused by several kinds of microorganisms. These microbes competed with the yeast that caused normal wine fermentation. Pasteur learned to predict a wine's taste just by identifying the microbes in a sample.

Once Pasteur knew what caused wine diseases, he began looking for a way to

Because France's economy was so dependent on the wine industry, the problem of spoiled wine was of national importance. Emperor Napoléon III asked Pasteur to find the causes and cures for "wine diseases."

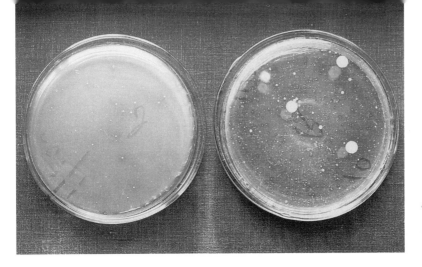

Two samples of bacteria growing in milk. The dish on the right contains unpasteurized milk and has much more bacterial growth.

prevent them. After many experiments, he found that heating wine to between 50 and 60 degrees Celsius (122 to 140 degrees Fahrenheit) for a few moments in the absence of air killed the unwanted microorganisms.

Many wine makers insisted at first that heating would ruin the taste of their wine. In reply, Pasteur invited professional wine tasters to sample heated and unheated wines and try to guess which was which. They found that the heated wines tasted better than the unheated ones.

Pasteurization

In a later test, samples of heated and unheated wine were placed aboard a ship that was going on a ten-month cruise. When the ship returned, the heated wine still had a fine flavor. The unheated wine, however, had become acid. These results suggested that heating would solve the costly problems that ruined French wine during shipping. Pasteur published the results of his work on wine in 1866.

Pasteur's technique for brief heating was soon named after him: pasteurization. He worked with manufacturers to design equipment that could carry out the process on large amounts of liquid at low cost. As he had done with his vinegar process, he patented pasteurization and then gave the patents to the public. The process soon became widespread. It saved French winemakers a huge amount of money.

Pasteurization was applied later in the century to other foods and beverages, including cheese, beer, vinegar, cider, and milk. The process did not kill all the microorganisms in these substances. Doing so would have been undesirable, because some types of organisms are needed for flavor. Pasteurization killed only the harmful microbes.

Pasteurization is still used, especially with milk. (The technique has changed slightly since Pasteur's time.) Besides slowing the spoilage of milk, pasteurization helps to prevent the spread of certain disease microbes that milk can carry. It thus makes milk safer to drink as well as longer lasting. Pasteurization was a gift not only to Pasteur's time but also to our own.

6 Silkworms and War

Pasteur received an impassioned letter from his old friend and teacher, Jean-Baptiste Dumas, early in 1865. "The distress is beyond anything you can imagine," Dumas's letter concluded.[52]

Dumas was talking about the misery of the silkworm breeders in the south of France. He said they were losing millions of francs a year because of a disease that attacked the silkworms. Dumas had been born in one of the silk-producing districts. He pleaded with Pasteur to find a way to prevent or combat the illness. The minister of agriculture added an official note to the plea. Pasteur had cured the diseases of wine. Dumas and the minister hoped he could cure sick silkworms as well.

"Your proposition throws me into a great perplexity," Pasteur answered Dumas. "I have never even touched a silkworm."[53] Still, he accepted the challenge. He wanted to help his friend and the unhappy silkworm breeders. He also hoped that learning about the silkworm disease would help him explore the relationship he thought might exist between disease and putrefaction. Many diseases broke down parts of the body while the victims were still alive, much as putrefaction did after death. Pasteur suspected that microbes

Silk workers gather leaves from mulberry trees and place the leaves on shelves to feed the silkworms.

Memories of Pont Gisquet

René Dubos, in his biography of Pasteur, describes the seasons of silkworm research at Pont Gisquet as a busy but happy time for Pasteur and his family.

"Everybody, including Madame Pasteur and the little Marie-Louise, engaged in the raising of the worms and in the collection and selection of the eggs. Countless experiments and microscopic examinations; painstaking control and watch over the trial cultures; worry over the ever-present threat of mice, which preferred silkworms to the most succulent baits; the feverish harvest of mulberry leaves when rain was threatening—all these occupations left, to those who participated in the work, the memory of laborious days, but also that of one of the happiest periods in the scientific life of the master. . . .

[Sending out eggs to *magnaneries* to be tested] soon led to an enormous volume of correspondence, which was handled by Pasteur himself. He spent his evenings dictating to his wife replies to distant collaborators, . . . articles for the trade journals, scientific articles for the academies and, finally, his book on the diseases of silkworms. . . .

A photograph of Pasteur dictating a scientific note to his wife in a garden, with a large sun hat in the background, calls forth a scene of olive trees and the brilliant skies of Provence, with cicadas humming their endless chant in the cool of the evening. It must have been good to work at Pont Gisquet, with an orangery for laboratory, and trees and water for office furniture."

Louis and Marie Pasteur at Pont Gisquet.

caused these diseases, just as they caused putrefaction.

Before going to see the sick silkworms, Pasteur read all he could about silkworm raising. He learned that French silkworm nurseries were called *magnaneries*. The breeders raised one brood a year, between April and June. The worms lived on tray-like beds. Attendants brought them fresh leaves from mulberry trees. These leaves were the only food the worms would eat.

Silkworms were really the caterpillars of a kind of moth. When the worms were ready to transform into moths, they wrapped themselves in cocoons of a silky material. This silk came from their heads as a single long thread. After a time, moths broke out of the cocoons and mated. The females then laid eggs. These eggs hatched into the next silkworm brood.

Thread from the silkworms' cocoons was made into silk cloth. The moths ruined the valuable thread when they broke out of the cocoons. The breeders therefore killed most of the worms with heat while they were still in their cocoons. Only a few moths were allowed to emerge and make eggs.

By the early nineteenth century, silk production had become one of France's most famous industries. Raising the silkworms and the leaves to feed them was so profitable that French people nicknamed the mulberry tree "the tree of gold." In a peak year, the French could produce 20 million kilograms of cocoons. The resulting silk was worth 100 million francs.

Pasteur learned that a strange disease had begun to kill huge numbers of French silkworms in 1845. The breeders called it *pébrine* or "pepper sickness." This name referred to tiny black spots, like grains of pepper, that often appeared on the sick worms.

By 1865 *pébrine* had spread throughout Europe. It even invaded China, where silkworm raising had begun. In France the sickness nearly wiped out the silk industry. As Pasteur later wrote in his book about silkworm diseases:

Now the mulberry plantations are abandoned, the "golden tree" no longer enriches the country, faces once beaming with health and good humour are now sad and drawn. Distress and hunger have succeeded to [replaced] comfort and happiness.[54]

Multiple Tragedies

Alais (now Alès) was a center of the silkworm industry in southeastern France. Pasteur went there in June 1865 to study worms with *pébrine*. He had been in the city only nine days, however, when he received word that his father was very ill. By the time Pasteur reached Arbois, Jean Joseph Pasteur was dead.

Jean Joseph's death was just the first of several losses Pasteur would suffer in the next year. In the fall of 1865, after Pasteur had returned to Paris from Alais, his youngest child, Camille, became ill. She may have had cancer. Pasteur sat up with her night after night, but she died in September. In February 1866, when he had returned to Alais and his wife and two remaining daughters were on their way to join him, twelve-year-old Cécile caught typhoid fever. She died on May 23. Only two of Pasteur's five children were now left: Jean-Baptiste, who was in college in Paris, and eight-year-old Marie-Louise.

Returning to Alais after his father's funeral in 1865, the grieving Pasteur tried to focus his mind on the puzzle of *pébrine*. He began by studying shiny, oval corpuscles (cells) that scientists had seen under the microscope when they looked at the bodies of diseased worms. He suspected that these corpuscles might be microorganisms that caused the disease.

His first experiments, however, seemed to disprove that idea. He found apparently healthy worms that were full of corpuscles. Other worms were obviously sick, yet did not contain the shiny bodies. Pasteur decided that *pébrine* was caused by a disturbance in the body of the worms. The corpuscles must be an effect, not a cause, of the disease.

In these beliefs he was mistaken. Still, just two weeks after starting his studies, Pasteur worked out a way to select silkworm eggs that was a great step toward preventing the disease. Breeders, he said, should look for corpuscles in each moth's body before deciding whether to keep its

Workers sort silkworm cocoons that will be spun into silk cloth. The silkworm diseases had a crippling effect on silk production.

eggs. If a moth contained many corpuscles, the disease would be passed on in its eggs. Worms born from such eggs would die before making their cocoons. If, however, a moth contained no corpuscles or only a few, it would lay healthy eggs. By throwing away eggs of moths with corpuscles, the breeders could keep *pébrine* from spreading to new broods of worms.

During the next three silkworm seasons, Pasteur lived in a large, pleasant house at Pont Gisquet, about a mile from Alais. His wife and daughter, as well as his assistants, also stayed there. The Pont Gisquet house became both a laboratory and a silkworm nursery. Everyone helped in the work, even Marie-Louise. When some silkworm breeders complained that learning to use a microscope to look for corpuscles was too hard, Pasteur replied, "There is in my laboratory a little girl eight years of age who has learned to use it without difficulty."[55]

Pasteur refined his method for selecting healthy silkworm eggs. At first he had looked for corpuscles in just a small part of each moth. He found, however, that the test was more accurate if the entire moth was examined. He used his test to select batches of healthy eggs, which he gave to other breeders. He also tested the breeders' eggs and predicted which batches would yield healthy worms. Almost all his predictions were correct.

Pasteur and his assistants showed that *pébrine* was highly contagious. It could be spread by mulberry leaves containing droppings from sick worms. It could invade the worms through breaks in the skin. But worms that picked up the disease by contagion, rather than being born with it, usually lived to spin successful cocoons. This meant that getting rid of infected

The microscope used by Pasteur during his research on silkworm diseases.

eggs ensured full silk production, even though it did not prevent all cases of the disease.

Some silkworm breeders adopted Pasteur's testing methods. Others, however, resented the idea of a mere chemist telling them what to do. Dealers in silkworm eggs were also angry with Pasteur because, if they followed his advice, they would have to throw most of their stock away. They spread false stories about him. One of these reached Marie Pasteur's father, who sent his daughter an alarmed letter in 1868. He had heard that "the failure of Pasteur's process has excited the population of your neighborhood so

much that he has had to flee from Alais, pursued by infuriated inhabitants throwing stones after him."[56]

"There Are Two Diseases!"

Pasteur received a setback in 1867, when worms from eggs he expected to be healthy began to die. He wrote:

> In a brood of a hundred worms, I picked up fifteen or twenty dead ones every day, black and rotting with extraordinary rapidity. . . . They were soft and flaccid [limp] like an empty bladder. I looked in vain for corpuscles; there was not a trace of them.[57]

Emile Duclaux described Pasteur's reaction to this new puzzle:

> We found our master more and more anxious. He kept us so remote from his thought that we could not explain his uneasiness till that day when he appeared before us almost in tears, and, dropping discouraged into a chair said: "Nothing is accomplished; there are two diseases!"[58]

The second disease was not really new. Silkworm breeders called it *flacherie*, 'the flatulent disease' because it gave the worms gassy diarrhea. Most scientists, however, had thought it was just a form of *pébrine*.

Pasteur's assistants soon persuaded him that he was wrong in believing that nothing had been accomplished by his research. The discovery that *flacherie* was a different disease from *pébrine* explained why some worms became sick even though they contained no *pébrine* corpuscles. Other mysteries were solved when experiments by Jean-Baptiste Gernez, one of Pasteur's assistants, finally convinced Pasteur that the mysterious corpuscles did cause *pébrine*. (They were protozoan microorganisms, which Pasteur had not worked with before.)

In the next several years, Pasteur showed that *flacherie*, like *pébrine*, is very contagious. It also can be passed from one generation to the next through the moths' eggs. Pasteur found bacteria associated with the disease, but these germs may not really cause it. René Dubos thinks the real cause of *flacherie* may be a virus that weakens the worms. The worms then fall prey to the bacteria.

Pasteur noticed that some environmental conditions increased worms' chances of getting *flacherie*. Crowding and

Drawings from one of Pasteur's books on the diseases of silkworms, in which he revealed methods of preventing these contagious diseases.

dampness were among these. Such conditions probably caused the bacteria to multiply. They most likely weakened the worms' resistance to disease as well. Pasteur told the breeders that providing a clean, open environment for the worms, as well as destroying infected eggs, would help to prevent *flacherie*.

A Frightening Stroke

In the fall of 1868, on the emperor's orders, workmen began to build a new, larger laboratory for Pasteur at the Ecole Normale. Pasteur was happy and excited as he watched the work. On the morning of October 19, however, he felt a strange tingling in his left side. This turned into a shivering fit by lunchtime. By evening his left side was paralyzed. Although Pasteur was only forty-five years old, a blood vessel in his brain had burst. He had had a stroke.

Pasteur lay close to death for weeks. "It is like lead," he complained of his paralyzed left arm. "If it could only be cut off!"[59] His mind, however, remained clear. "Would willingly talk science," his doctor noted two days after the stroke.[60]

"All scientific Paris comes to inquire anxiously after the patient," a cousin wrote during this time.[61] Even the emperor sent a servant to Pasteur's home daily for news of Pasteur's health.

The news slowly improved. On November 30 Pasteur was able to sit up in an armchair for the first time. During the next year or so, most movement returned to his left side. In time, he had only a slight limp and some stiffness in his left hand.

On January 18, just three months after the stroke, Pasteur returned to Alais. His friends and family tried to make him rest. (He wrote to Dumas that Marie-Louise "pitilessly takes books, pens, papers and pencils away from me with a perseverance which causes me joy and despair."[62]) With the help of his assistants, he nonetheless continued his silkworm research.

The Franco-Prussian War

Pasteur published a two-volume book on the diseases of silkworms in 1870. By then the silkworm plague was mostly controlled. Pasteur's beloved homeland, however, now faced a greater danger—war. Otto von Bismarck, the chancellor (prime minister) of the state of Prussia, had united several small German states under Prussia's leadership. This group, the North German Federation, was the beginning of the modern nation of Germany. Bismarck built up the federation's army and prepared it for war against France. The French, under the weak leadership of Napoléon III, were badly outnumbered and unready for a fight.

The Franco-Prussian War began in July 1870. Pasteur's eighteen-year-old son, Jean-Baptiste, was one of many soldiers who fought in it. On September 1 the Germans defeated a large French force at Sedan and captured Napoléon III. Hearing the news, crowds in Paris revolted against imperial rule. As in 1848, they set up a republican government. This government continued the war.

The French expected the Germans to soon surround and attack Paris. Pasteur wanted to remain in the city. Friends, however, persuaded him to go to Arbois, where one of his sisters still lived. Furious at everything German, Pasteur vowed that "every one of my future works will bear on its title page the words, 'Hatred to Prussia. Revenge! revenge!'"[63]

After four months of siege, Paris surrendered to the Germans late in January 1871. A treaty ended the war on March 1. The treaty ordered France to pay large sums of money to Germany. France also

A devastated Paris, as it looked in 1871 after the Franco-Prussian War. For a while after the war, German armies occupied the part of France where Pasteur had been living. Pasteur left the area to stay with a friend in the town of Clermont.

Seeking a Son

After Pasteur heard that Jean-Baptiste had been involved in a battle that had gone badly for the French, he and his wife set off in a broken-down carriage to look for their son. In his Life of Pasteur, *René Vallery-Radot described the family's reunion.*

"The town was full of soldiers, some crouching round fires in the street, others stepping across their dead horses and begging for a little straw to lie on. Many had taken refuge in the church and were lying on the steps of the altar; a few were attempting to bandage their frozen feet. . . .

'All that I can tell you,' said a soldier anxiously questioned by Mme. [Madame] Pasteur, 'is that out of the 1,200 men of that battalion there are but 300 left.' As she was questioning another, a soldier who was passing stopped: 'Sergeant Pasteur? Yes, he is alive; I slept by him last night at Chaffois. He has remained behind; he is ill. You might meet him on the road towards Chaffois.'

The Pasteurs started again on the road followed the day before. They had barely passed the Pontarlier gate when a rough cart came by. A soldier muffled in his great coat, his hands resting on the edge of the cart, started with surprise. He hurried down, and the family embraced without a word, so great was their emotion."

had to give Germany the territory of Alsace and part of the territory of Lorraine.

The Prussians took over Arbois, south of Lorraine, for a while after the war, so Pasteur could not remain there. He wanted to return to Paris, but his friends advised him not to do so. Parisians were protesting the terms of the peace treaty and trying to change the country's government once again. As a result, civil war was raging through the city. Pasteur therefore decided to visit his former assistant, Emile Duclaux, at Clermont-Ferrand University. Duclaux taught chemistry there.

While staying with Duclaux, Pasteur launched into a new project: the study of beer. Both Germany and France made beer, but most people thought German beer was better. Pasteur wanted to help his country by reversing that situation. To find out how beer was made and what made it taste good, he first visited a brewery near Clermont. Then, in September 1871, he traveled to a large brewery in London.

Pasteur placed several samples of the London brewers' beer under his microscope. He then amazed the brewers by announcing that the beer was spoiled or soon would become so. The brewery managers reluctantly admitted he was right. Pasteur showed the brewers the microorganisms that had warned him the beer was bad. "When I returned to the same brewery less than a week later," he later recalled, "I learned that the managers had made haste to acquire a microscope and to change all the yeasts which were in operation at the time of my first visit."[64]

Pasteur showed that beer, like wine, spoiled because microbes invaded the mixture and competed with the yeast in it. These problems could be prevented by using a microscope to look for such microorganisms in samples of the beer. Keeping germ-carrying dust and air out of the mixture was also important. Finally, Pasteur recommended that the beer be pasteurized. He showed that this heat treatment could destroy unwanted microbes in beer, just as it did in wine.

Following his London trip, Pasteur went back to Paris. By then peace had returned to the city. (The government had suppressed the citizens' rebellion in late May.) Back in his old laboratory at the Ecole Normale, Pasteur continued his work on beer until 1877. He learned more about microorganisms and fermentation, but he never succeeded in making French beer better than German beer.

Microbes and Disease

Even Pasteur's research on beer kept him thinking of the more important puzzle that had concerned him for years: the relationship between microorganisms and disease. He wrote:

> When we see beer and wine subjected to deep alterations because they have given refuge to micro-organisms invisibly introduced and now swarming

Pasteur's apparatus for cooling and fermenting beer. Pasteur recommended pasteurizing beer to kill unwanted microbes.

within them, it is impossible not to be pursued by the thought that similar facts may, *must*, take place in animals and in man.[65]

Pasteur had shown that microbes could cause disease in silkworms. He believed that they could also do this in higher animals and human beings. The diseases that microbes seemed most likely to cause were contagious diseases, those that spread from one living thing to another.

Some scientists before Pasteur's time had guessed that contagious diseases might be caused by tiny living things. Even after Leeuwenhoek's microscope revealed that such "little animals" really existed, however, no one had proved that they caused any serious human disease. Pasteur hoped to prove that microbes could cause human diseases. Better still, he hoped to find a way to prevent these diseases.

Chapter

7 Miracles on the Farm

The first contagious disease Pasteur worked with was not primarily a human disease, although humans could catch it. It mostly affected sheep, cows, and similar domestic animals. The disease was called anthrax, which means 'coal' in Greek. It was given this name because the blood of animals that died of it was clotted and coal-black. Loss of animals from anthrax cost farmers in some parts of France as much as 20 million francs in bad years. They sometimes lost half their sheep flocks to the disease.

Little Rods

Some veterinarians saw "little rods" in the blood of anthrax-infected animals as early as 1838. A veterinarian named Davaine noticed that the rods were much like the microorganisms that made butyric acid in Pasteur's experiments. Davaine suggested in 1863 that the rodlike microbes might cause anthrax. Other scientists, however, disagreed. For example, two researchers named Jaillard and Leplat claimed they had caused anthrax in rabbits by injecting them with blood from a cow that died of the disease. Yet, they said, the rods did not appear in the rabbits' blood. Jaillard and Leplat did not know what caused anthrax, but they claimed it could not be the rods.

In 1876 a German scientist, Robert Koch, found a way to grow the rodlike microbes in nutrient fluids. (Koch contributed as much as Pasteur to the study of disease microorganisms.) He worked out the life cycle of these microorganisms. He showed that they could form spores that resisted heat and chemicals. The spores could survive for years. Under the right

The "little rods" that Pasteur and other scientists found in anthrax-infected animals can be seen in this blood sample.

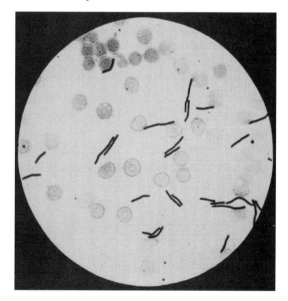

German scientist Robert Koch discovered the microbes that cause the dreaded disease anthrax.

conditions, they turned back into active microbes.

Koch injected pure cultures of the rodlike microbes into animals. The animals promptly died of anthrax. These and other experiments proved that the little rods caused the disease. Thus Koch beat Pasteur to the goal of showing that microbes could cause disease in higher animals. Koch's work was not widely accepted at first, however. Many veterinarians resisted the new idea that microbes could cause disease.

When Pasteur started his research on anthrax, he knew of Davaine's experiments but not, at first, of Koch's. He therefore unintentionally repeated some of Koch's work. Like Koch, he concluded that the rodlike germs caused anthrax.

Pasteur also answered some of the veterinarians' objections. He said that the animals injected by Jaillard and Leplat, for example, had not died of anthrax at all. Jaillard and Leplat had used blood from animals that died a day or more before they injected it. Pasteur showed that for the first few hours after death, the blood of anthrax-infected animals contained only the rodlike microbes. Blood from animals that had died a day or more before, however, also contained microbes that he called septic vibrios. The older the blood, the more septic vibrios and fewer rods were in it. When Pasteur injected pure cultures of septic vibrios into animals, the animals died of a disease like the one Jaillard and Leplat had described.

Cursed Fields

Farmers knew that animals grazing in certain fields were almost sure to get anthrax, while others in nearby pastures stayed healthy. The farmers said such fields were cursed. The "curse," Pasteur quickly learned, was that animals that had died of anthrax were buried in the fatal fields. He and his assistants found spores of anthrax microbes in the soil of the fields. Later they showed that these spores could stay in the soil twelve years after an anthrax-infected animal was buried there. When revived, the spores produced the disease.

In 1878, Pasteur's research on anthrax led the minister of agriculture to ask him to try to find a way of preventing or curing the disease. Pasteur sent two assistants, Charles Chamberland and Emile Roux, to the areas of France most affected by anthrax. The two conducted experiments on farms every summer for several years. Pasteur joined them once a week to review their work and suggest new experiments. "What pleasant memories we have kept of the campaign against anthrax in the

Keen Eyes Make a Discovery

Emile Roux, Pasteur's assistant, once described how Pasteur made an important discovery about how anthrax is spread. René Dubos quotes Roux in his biography of Pasteur.

"On the days when Pasteur came to Chartres, . . . [he] would hasten to the sheep [pens]. Motionless near the gates, he would observe the experimental animals with that sustained attention from which nothing could escape; for hours in succession, he would keep his gaze fastened on a sheep that he thought diseased. We had to remind him of the hour and show him that the spires of the Chartres cathedral were beginning to fade into the night before he could make up his mind to leave. . . .

Pasteur . . . knew how to draw the most unexpected leads from the smallest detail. The original idea of the role of earthworms in the dissemination [spread] of anthrax was thus born one day when we were walking through a field. . . . Pasteur's attention was drawn to a part of the field where the earth was of different color. . . . [The field's owner] explained that sheep dead of anthrax had been buried there the preceding year. Pasteur . . . noticed at the surface a multitude of those small casts of soil such as are ejected by earthworms. He then conceived the idea that in their endless trips from the lower levels, the worms bring up the anthrax spores present in the earth . . . that surrounds the cadavers [corpses]. Pasteur never stopped at ideas, but immediately proceeded to the experiment. . . . The earth extracted from the intestine of one of the worms, injected into guinea pigs, forthwith gave them anthrax."

Chartres country!" Roux wrote later. "How interesting and healthy was this bacteriology [study of bacteria] in the open air!"[66]

These field experiments cleared up several mysteries about the way anthrax was spread. For example, Pasteur and his assistants tried to give anthrax to sheep and cattle by putting anthrax spores on their food. Many of the animals stayed healthy. If the food included prickly plants such as thistles, however, the animals quickly became ill. Pasteur guessed that the anthrax germs invaded the animals' blood through the tiny cuts in their mouths made by this food.

At the same time Pasteur was studying anthrax, he was trying to convince doctors that microbes might cause human disease.

Antiseptic Surgery

Joseph Lister published On the Antiseptic Principle of the Practice of Surgery *in 1867. An extract from Lister's book appears in Samuel Rapport and Helen Wright's* Great Adventures in Medicine. *In this excerpt, Lister tells how Pasteur's research on microbes in the air gave him the idea for using antiseptics, or microbe-killing chemicals, to prevent infection of wounds after injury or surgery.*

"To prevent . . . suppuration [infection of wounds] . . . till lately . . . [appeared] unattainable, since it seemed hopeless to attempt to exclude the oxygen which was universally regarded as the agent by which putrefaction was effected [caused]. But when it had been shown by the researches of Pasteur that the septic [harmfully infectious] properties of the atmosphere depended not on the oxygen . . . but on minute organisms suspended in it, . . . it occurred to me that decomposition in the injured part might be avoided without excluding the air, by applying as a dressing some material capable of destroying the life of the floating particles. . . .

The material which I have employed is carbolic or phenic acid, . . . which appears to exercise a peculiarly destructive influence upon low forms of life. . . .

I have now under my care . . . a boy who was admitted [to the hospital] with compound fracture of the leg [a broken leg in which one end of the bone had broken through the skin] . . . eight and one-half hours after the accident, in whom, nevertheless, all local and constitutional disturbance [all infection of the wound or general illness] was avoided by means of carbolic acid, and the bones were soundly united five weeks after his admission."

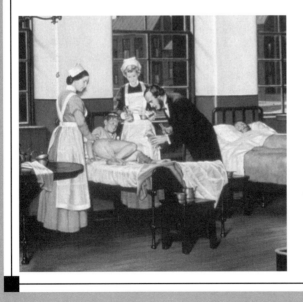

Joseph Lister treats a patient's wounds with antiseptic. Pasteur's research on microbes had inspired Lister to investigate the use of antiseptics to kill unwanted microbes and prevent infection.

A few far-sighted doctors were willing to consider this possibility. In 1874, for example, Pasteur received a letter from Joseph Lister, an English surgeon working in Scotland. In it, Lister commended Pasteur:

> Allow me to . . . tender [offer] you my most cordial thanks for having, by your brilliant researches, demonstrated to me the truth of the germ theory of putrefaction, and thus furnished me with the principle upon which alone [my] antiseptic system can be carried out.[67]

Lister had read Pasteur's reports about the microbes that lived in air and dust. He had also studied the paper in which Pasteur showed that germs living without oxygen caused putrefaction. Like Pasteur, Lister believed that some diseases were a kind of putrefaction of living animals. He thought the wound infections that often killed people after injuries or surgical operations were among these diseases.

If microbes caused wound infections, Lister reasoned, such infections might be prevented by killing microbes in the wounds. He used a powerful chemical to do this. He described his antiseptic, or microbe-killing, technique in a book. He sent a copy of the book to Pasteur along with his letter.

A small number of French doctors began to use techniques like Lister's. Most physicians, however, resisted the idea that microbes could cause disease. This new theory countered everything they had learned. They had been taught that disease spread from sick to healthy matter by some kind of chemical process, as Liebig thought about fermentation.

Doctors also resisted the germ theory of disease because it suggested that they were unintentionally harming their patients. Doctors in hospitals treated one patient after another without washing their hands or changing clothes. If disease-causing microbes existed in infected matter, the doctors were spreading the deadly germs from one patient to the next. Most doctors were unwilling to admit that they could be doing such a terrible thing.

"I Shall Force Them to See"

As a leading supporter of the germ theory, Pasteur argued constantly with doctors who opposed it. He had become an associate member of the Academy of Medicine in 1873. Academy meetings he attended almost always ended in a shouting match. The academy doctors never let Pasteur forget that he was a chemist, not a physician. Pasteur, in turn, scolded the doctors for their poor scientific knowledge. "I shall force them to see; they will have to see!" he raged to his assistants when he returned from one of these meetings.[68]

Pasteur's most important battle with the doctors took place at an academy meeting in March 1878. During the meeting, one doctor gave a long description of the possible causes of childbirth fever. This disease killed many women just after they had given birth, especially if they went to a hospital to have their babies. In the early 1840s, Oliver Wendell Holmes in the United States and Ignaz Semmelweis in Hungary had suggested that childbirth fever was spread from woman to woman by the dirty hands of doctors or midwives. (Midwives were nurses who helped during the birth process.) The two doctors had not been able to prove this claim, however.

Most other physicians ignored or made fun of them.

Pasteur believed that childbirth fever must be caused by microbes. These, he thought, were what the doctors and midwives spread. To support his idea, he made cultures of matter taken from infected women. In these cultures he found round microbes that grew in chains. (Today they are called streptococcus, a kind of bacteria.) He concluded that these microbes usually caused childbirth fever.

As the March academy meeting wore on, Pasteur found he could no longer stand the doctor's boring—and mistaken—lecture. "None of those things cause the epidemic," he broke in. "It is the nursing and medical staff who carry the microbe from an infected woman to a healthy one." The elderly doctor who had been interrupted said he doubted that he would live long enough to see such a microbe discovered. In reply, Pasteur strode to the blackboard and drew his chainlike bacteria. "There, that is what it is like!" he shouted.[69]

A Mistake Leads to a Discovery

As if arguing with doctors, visiting hospitals, and guiding his assistants' research on anthrax were not enough, Pasteur began studying another animal disease in 1879. This illness was chicken cholera. It sometimes killed 90 percent of a farmer's flock in a few days. Sick birds fluffed their feathers into a ball, fell into a deep sleep, and died. A veterinarian named Toussaint had discovered the germ that caused the disease. He suggested that Pasteur do further research on it.

In the summer of 1880, before leaving for his vacation, Pasteur told his assistant Charles Chamberland to inject some chickens with a culture of chicken cholera bacteria. Chamberland may have been in a hurry to begin his own holidays. In any case, he forgot Pasteur's orders. The culture stayed in the lab for a month.

When Chamberland returned and carried out the delayed injections, he found a surprise. The injected chickens fell ill briefly, then recovered. For some reason, the old culture's virulence, or disease-causing power, had decreased greatly. Chamberland was about to throw the culture away, but Pasteur stopped him. Pasteur suggested injecting the recovered chickens with a batch of new, strong culture. To the amazement of everyone—except perhaps Pasteur—the chickens did not become sick. Yet new chickens injected with the same fresh culture died as usual. The old, weak culture had somehow protected the chickens from the powerful one. Pasteur knew that this kind of thing sometimes happened in nature. For example, he had seen a few sheep recover from anthrax. They then failed to get the disease again, even when exposed to large doses of anthrax spores.

People long before Pasteur's time had noticed that some contagious diseases could be caught only once. This fact had been used to prevent one fatal disease, smallpox. In the late 1700s, an English country doctor named Edward Jenner saw that women who milked cows often got a rash called cowpox. Cowpox seemed like smallpox but was much milder. A few of the women told Jenner that anyone who had had cowpox could not get smallpox. After many years he became convinced that they were right. In 1796 Jenner deliberately

Edward Jenner vaccinates an eight-year-old boy against smallpox. After receiving an injection of cowpox, the boy became ill with the disease. Jenner then injected him with smallpox, but he remained healthy. The vaccine was a success.

gave a boy cowpox and then scratched matter from a smallpox sore into his skin. The boy did not get smallpox. Jenner called his process *vaccination*, from the Latin name for cowpox. He published a report of his work in an important scientific journal in 1798. The practice of vaccination soon spread, and it saved many lives.

Pasteur had Jenner's work in mind as he watched the healthy chickens that should have died. Jenner had stumbled onto an existing disease that protected people against another, more serious disease. Most contagious diseases, however, lacked such harmless "twins." But what if a harmless or nearly harmless material, something like cowpox matter, could be created in the laboratory and then used for protection? Pasteur believed he had found a way to do this. To honor Jenner, he used the word *vaccination* for the process of putting weakened germs into the body to build up resistance or immunity to a disease.

Pasteur and his assistants began experiments to confirm and expand their chick-

en cholera discovery. They let cultures of the disease bacteria age, in the presence of oxygen, for different numbers of days. They found that the cultures became steadily weaker as they grew older. After they reached a certain age, the germs were unable to cause disease at all. Furthermore, if cultures at any particular stage of weakness were returned to normal care, in which the medium was renewed with fresh nutrients, they kept the same degree of virulence. Pasteur and his assistants showed that they could inject chickens with a weak culture and later with a full-strength culture, and the chickens would remain healthy. In short, by the end of 1880 Pasteur had developed a vaccine for chicken cholera.

Drama at Pouilly le Fort

If he could create a vaccine to protect against one disease caused by microbes, Pasteur was sure he could do the same for others. His mind turned at once to anthrax, which he was still studying. He first tried to weaken anthrax bacteria by aging cultures in air, the method that had worked for chicken cholera. Instead of becoming weaker, however, the anthrax microbes simply formed spores. Finally, after many experiments, Pasteur found that if the anthrax bacteria were cultured at a temperature of 42 degrees Celsius (107.6 degrees Fahrenheit), they grew but did not make spores.

At this temperature, the anthrax bacteria acted like those of chicken cholera. The longer a culture was kept without changing the medium, the weaker the culture became. A culture ten or twelve days old made sheep only slightly ill. It also protected them from full-strength anthrax.

A "Stunning Success"

Pasteur let some of the weakened anthrax cultures cool off and form spores. He found that these spores, like the germs they came from, produced a mild and protective illness. The spores were easy to store and ship. Pasteur could now make and distribute large amounts of anthrax vaccine. He announced his results to the Academy of Sciences on February 28, 1881. He added that he hoped to make large-scale tests of the vaccine soon.

He had his chance sooner than he might have expected—thanks to a man who hoped he would fail. A veterinarian named Rossignol was one of many who thought Pasteur's germ theory was greatly overrated. Rossignol wrote sarcastically in the January 1881 *Veterinary Press*, "microbiolatry [worship of microbes] is the fash-

ion. . . . The Microbe alone is true, and Pasteur is its prophet."[70] In the spring of 1881, Rossingnol collected money to pay for a public test of Pasteur's anthrax vaccine. The test would be held at Pouilly le Fort, a farm that Rossignol owned near Melun.

Pasteur agreed to Rossignol's terms. Chamberland and Roux wondered whether Pasteur should have taken such a gamble. Rossignol had publicized the test widely. If the vaccine failed, all of Europe would hear about it. But Pasteur seemed to have no doubts. "What succeeded with fourteen sheep in the laboratory will succeed with fifty in Melun," he said firmly.[71]

Pasteur and his assistants injected twenty-four sheep, one goat, and six cows with weakened anthrax bacteria on May 5. On May 17, Roux and Chamberland gave the animals a second dose, made from a stronger culture. The vaccinated animals received injections of virulent anthrax bacteria on May 31. So did twenty-four sheep, one goat, and four cows that had not been vaccinated. Everyone was to gather on June 2 to see the result.

On June 1, Roux and Chamberland returned to Paris. They told Pasteur that some of the vaccinated sheep were ill. Until then Pasteur had shown only confidence in the results of the experiment. For a moment, however, tension overcame him. He turned on poor Roux, shouting that Roux had ruined the test through carelessness.

At the end of a long, sleepless night, Pasteur received a telegram saying that the vaccinated animals were better. His faith restored, he went with his family and assistants to Pouilly le Fort. He arrived to find all the vaccinated animals healthy. Twenty-one of the unvaccinated sheep and the unvaccinated goat, however, were already dead. Two more sheep died in front of the spectators' eyes. The last one died before the end of the day. The four unvaccinated cows, too, were sick. Even Rossignol admitted that Pasteur had scored a *stunning success.*[72] Roux's account of the experiment concluded that "in the multitude at Pouilly le Fort, that day, there were no longer any skeptics but only admirers."[73]

Newspaper reports spread the news of Pasteur's success all over Europe. Thousands of farmers began demanding the new vaccine. Pasteur said later that his group vaccinated twenty thousand sheep, as well as a great many oxen, cows, and horses, in a two-week period in the area around Paris alone.

This high demand caused problems. Chamberland and Roux struggled to mass-produce the vaccine. Exhausted and working with hastily made equipment, they did not always follow Pasteur's careful methods. Their vaccine sometimes was too weak. Sometimes it was contaminated with other microorganisms. This drew criticism both from unhappy farmers and from Pasteur's scientific rival, Robert Koch.

These problems were soon corrected, however. A report in 1894 stated that by then, 3.4 million sheep and 438,000 cattle had been vaccinated. The death rate was

Pasteur's assistants inject a sheep with the anthrax bacteria. After the success of Pasteur's vaccinating experiment, thousands of farmers began demanding the vaccine for their animals.

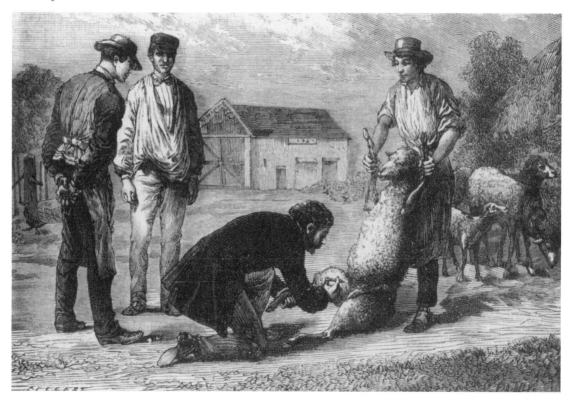

only 1 percent for sheep and 0.3 percent for cattle. The report estimated that the vaccine had saved French agriculture 5 million francs for the sheep and 2 million francs for the cattle. According to Réne Dubos, "It was the vaccination against anthrax that revealed to the medical community and lay [untrained] mind the practical possibilities of the new science of immunity."[74]

Savior of Humanity

Pasteur's fame had been growing steadily for years, and his work had won many prizes. Now he found himself famous to a degree he could hardly believe. In August 1881, two months after the test at Pouilly le Fort, he attended the International Medical Congress in London as France's representative. His son, Jean-Baptiste, and his son-in-law, René Vallery-Radot, went with him. (Both Jean-Baptiste and Marie-Louise had married in 1879.)

Vallery-Radot wrote about the trip in his biography of Pasteur. He said that when Pasteur entered St. James's Hall for the opening of the congress, a steward led him to the platform where the most important members were seated. As Pasteur walked toward the platform, applause and cheers spread through the packed hall.

"It is no doubt the Prince of Wales arriving," Pasteur murmured. "I ought to have come sooner."

Sir James Paget, the president of the congress, heard Pasteur's remark. "But it is you that they are all cheering," he told the startled scientist.[75]

Pasteur's own country heaped honors on him as well. In July 1881, the French government awarded him the Great Ribbon of the Legion of Honor. Roux and Chamberland were given red ribbons, the lesser award that Pasteur had won earlier. Pasteur had insisted that they be honored in this way. Marie Pasteur wrote to her children that "hearty congratulations were exchanged in the midst of the rabbits and guinea-pigs" when the group heard about the awards.[76]

Soon afterward, on December 8, 1881, Pasteur was elected a member of the French Academy of Letters (Académie Française). The academy had only forty members. They were the country's most esteemed men in all fields, from science to literature and politics.

More touching were the honors that came from the silk makers, wine and beer producers, farmers, and others whose livelihood Pasteur had saved. Some French towns named streets or schools after Pasteur. Others made medals or set up statues. The province of Cantal, for example, gave Pasteur a medal as part of an agricultural show in June 1883. As Pasteur was walking down the street after the ceremony, Vallery-Radot reports, a farmer hailed him, waving a large hat. When Pasteur stopped, the man vigorously shook his hand. "Long live Pasteur! You have saved my cattle," the farmer said simply.[77]

It was not surprising that Pasteur received letters from all types of people, begging him to find a cure or a vaccine for this or that disease. Many of these people thought he was a medical doctor. His friends sometimes had to explain that this image was wrong. "He does not cure individuals," one friend said to a foreigner who asked him about Pasteur's medical skills. "He only tries to cure humanity."[78]

Pasteur's major attempt to cure a human disease, though, was still to come.

Chapter

8 The Conquest of Rabies

Pasteur never forgot the terror that had swept through Arbois in 1831, when he was nine years old. Shouts and screams had brought him to the blacksmith's shop one day. There he learned that a wolf had bitten several townspeople. The people of Arbois knew that the wolf's furious attack and the white foam dripping from its mouth meant that the animal had rabies. The wolf's bites could give the painful disease to the people who had been attacked. The only treatment was to burn their wounds with a hot iron. Young Louis watched the blacksmith do this to a farmer named Nicole. The treatment saved Nicole, but eight others bitten by the wolf died of rabies. For months the people of Arbois lived in fear that the rabid wolf would return and attack again.

These memories surely rose into Pasteur's mind when he saw the strange "gift" brought to his laboratory one day in 1880. An army veterinary surgeon named Bourrel had sent him two rabid dogs! Bourrel had tried for years without success to find a treatment for rabies. He hoped the great Pasteur would have better luck.

Pasteur had just discovered his vaccine for chicken cholera. He and his assistants were still studying anthrax as well. He

A boy struggles with a rabid dog. Pasteur's frightening childhood memories of a rabid wolf that attacked several people in his town made him determined to find a treatment for rabies.

Concern for Animals

Some people called Pasteur a "laboratory executioner" because he used animals in his research. René Vallery-Radot reports, however, that Pasteur "had a great horror of inflicting suffering on any animal." In this excerpt, Vallery-Radot quotes Emile Roux, who described Pasteur's reaction after Roux operated on a dog's brain.

"[Pasteur] could assist without too much effort at a single operation such as a subcutaneous inoculation [injection under the skin], and even then, if the animal screamed at all, Pasteur was immediately filled with compassion, and tried to comfort and encourage the victim, in a way which would have seemed ludicrous [silly] if it had not been touching. The thought of having a dog's cranium [top of the skull] perforated was very disagreeable to him; he very much wished that the experiment should take place, and yet he feared to see it begun. I performed it one day when he was out. The next day, as I was telling him that the intercranial [into the brain] inoculation had presented no difficulty, he began pitying the dog. 'Poor thing! His brain is no doubt injured, he must be paralysed!' I did not answer, but went to fetch the dog, whom I brought into the laboratory. Pasteur was not fond of dogs, but when he saw this one, full of life, curiously investigating every part of the laboratory, he showed the keenest pleasure, and spoke to the dog in the most affectionate manner."

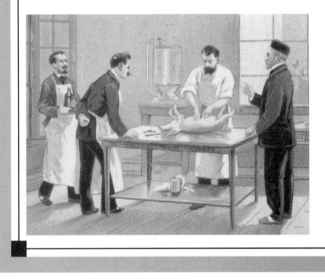

Pasteur uses a piglet in his research on measles. According to his assistant, Pasteur was compassionate with his experimental animals.

hardly appeared to have time for another disease. If he did take on a new project, rabies would seem an unlikely choice. The disease killed only a few hundred people in France each year. Most of those deaths probably could have been prevented by better control of stray dogs, the most common carriers of rabies.

Still, Pasteur knew that rabies was an illness everyone feared. The appearance of rabies victims was terrifying, and rabies was always fatal. Many people bitten by rabid animals did not develop rabies. Once signs of the disease appeared, however, death was certain.

Rabies, then, satisfied what René Dubos calls "Pasteur's longing for romantic problems."[79] It offered a great challenge to his scientific skills, since no one knew what caused it. Pasteur also may have sensed that a victory over rabies would do even more to spread his ideas and fame than the well-reported success at Pouilly le Fort. All these thoughts, along with his frightening childhood memories, probably helped him decide to follow Bourrel's suggestion.

Pasteur's desire to cure rabies must have grown in December 1880, when he saw his first human rabies victim. She was a five-year-old girl. René Vallery-Radot described her situation:

> The unfortunate little patient presented all the characteristics of hydrophobia ["fear of water," another name for human rabies]: spasms, restlessness, shudders at the least breath of air, an ardent [powerful] thirst, accompanied with an absolute impossibility of swallowing, convulsive movements, fits of furious rage. . . . The child died after twenty-four hours of horrible suffering—suffocated by the mucus which filled the mouth.[80]

Futile Search

Because rabies was spread by bites, whatever caused the disease seemed sure to be in the saliva of its victims. Pasteur therefore injected some of the dead girl's saliva into rabbits. Sure enough, the rabbits died within thirty-six hours. Their saliva, in turn, caused equally rapid death when injected into other rabbits. Pasteur found a microbe in the saliva and grew it in culture. When he injected the pure culture into rabbits, it too caused death.

At first Pasteur thought he was well on his way to finding the cause of rabies. But his careful observations did not let him fool himself for long. In both humans and

Pasteur makes notes on the condition of the caged rabbits that are part of his rabies experiments. Finding a treatment for rabies offered Pasteur a great chance to test his scientific skills.

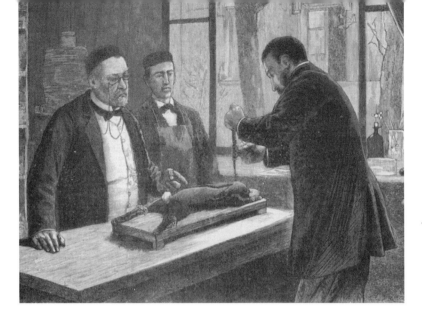

Pasteur watches as his assistant Emile Roux infects a healthy rabbit with rabid brain tissue to see if this will cause the animal to develop rabies.

dogs, he knew, the signs of rabies usually appeared weeks after a bite. The injected rabbits died much faster than that. They also failed to show the expected signs of rabies.

Pasteur began to suspect that the microbe he had found was giving the rabbits some disease other than rabies. He confirmed his guesses by finding the microbe in saliva from children who had died of other diseases. He even found it in a healthy adult. After months of further experiments, Pasteur finally decided that the microbe that caused rabies must be too small to see. (His guess was correct—the disease is caused by a virus. Scientists were able to see viruses only after the electron microscope was invented around 1930.)

Pasteur found he could not grow the rabies agent in any kind of nutrient medium. In order to study the agent, he therefore needed a dependable way to produce the disease in animals. He sometimes succeeded in giving rabies to rabbits by injecting the saliva of rabid dogs. Often, however, this method did not work. Since the signs of rabies showed that the disease affected the brain, he tried using bits of rabid dogs' brains instead. When injected under the skin, the brain tissue worked better than saliva, but not much.

Emile Roux then suggested putting the rabid brain tissue directly on a healthy dog's brain. This could be done by making a small hole in the skull, an operation called trephining. The operation would be done under anesthesia, so the animal would feel no pain.

Roux, a medical doctor, trephined his first dog on May 6, 1881. This was the day after he had given the first anthrax vaccinations at Pouilly le Fort. The dog developed rabies after just two weeks. Further experiments showed that this way of producing rabies was dependable and fast. It worked in both dogs and rabbits.

Making a Vaccine

Pasteur wanted to create a vaccine for rabies. He hoped to make one that could be given to people after they had been bitten by rabid animals. The fact that signs of rabies usually appeared several weeks after a bite suggested that a vaccine would have time to keep the disease from developing.

In order to make a vaccine, Pasteur had to find a way to weaken the virus. Growing the virus in monkeys sometimes produced this effect, but not always. Pasteur searched for a better method.

Some of Emile Roux's experiments gave Pasteur the idea he needed. While working on rabies, Roux had invented a new kind of flask with two openings. The openings were closed with plugs of cotton wool. Roux hung a rabbit spinal cord from

A flask used by Pasteur contains a dried rabbit spinal cord that was used in creating a rabies vaccine.

the plug that closed the flask's top opening. This design kept out dust and germs but allowed air to flow around the cord.

Adrien Loir, Pasteur's nephew, was with Pasteur when Pasteur saw one of Roux's new flasks for the first time. Loir later wrote:

> At the sight of this flask, Pasteur became so absorbed in his thoughts that I did not dare disturb him. . . . After remaining silent and motionless a long time, Pasteur took the flask outside, looked at it, then returned it to its place without saying a word.[81]

Pasteur then told Loir to get the glass blower to make more flasks like Roux's.

Pasteur used the new flasks to age rabid spinal cords in contact with air, much as he had done with the chicken cholera germs. He then injected dried, ground-up cords of different ages into dogs. He found that the virulence of the cords decreased day by day. Injections of fresh cords always produced rabies. Two-week-old cords, however, caused no illness.

Pasteur now used these dried cords to build up dogs' resistance to rabies. Each dog received a two-week series of injections under the skin. The injections started with two-week-old cord. They progressed to thirteen-day-old cord on the next day, and so on. On the last day, they used cord from a freshly killed rabid rabbit.

After vaccinating the dogs, Pasteur tested their immunity. He placed virulent rabies tissue into the brains of some and let rabid dogs bite others. The treated dogs stayed healthy. Pasteur demonstrated his first vaccinated dogs in mid-1884.

As soon as Pasteur's vaccine began to produce dependable results in dogs, people started asking him whether he was

Pasteur injected dogs with increasingly stronger doses of rabies to see if they developed resistance to the disease.

ready to use the vaccine on human beings. For about a year he said no. He wanted to be very sure of his results in animals first. He hesitated even after he showed that his vaccine could protect dogs if they received it after being bitten by a rabid animal.

Then circumstances forced his hand. On July 6, 1885, a terrified nine-year-old boy named Joseph Meister entered Pasteur's laboratory. His mother came with him. The Meisters lived in Alsace, she said. A rabid dog had attacked Joseph when he was on his way to school two days before. The dog bit him fourteen times on the hands and legs. Some of the bites were so deep that the boy could hardly walk. That evening a local doctor washed out the wounds with carbolic acid, the same powerful antiseptic Joseph Lister used. He then recommended that the Meisters see Pasteur, whose rabies experiments he had heard about.

When Pasteur heard the boy's story, his anguish became almost as great as the

Meisters'. What should he do? He still was unsure whether his vaccine was ready to be used on humans. But Joseph's bites were many and deep. They meant that the boy was almost sure to get rabies if he was not treated. Pasteur sought the advice of two physician friends, Edme Vulpian and Jacques Grancher. After examining Joseph, both agreed that giving the vaccine was the only way to save the boy's life.

As Vulpian and Grancher watched, Pasteur gave Joseph Meister his first injection. In contained a small amount of fifteen-day-old rabbit spinal cord in liquid. During the next ten days Joseph received twelve more injections. Each contained fresher and more virulent cord than the one before.

Pasteur arranged for Joseph and his mother to stay in rooms nearby. As the days passed, the boy played happily in the laboratory among the chickens, rabbits, and other animals. He had a good appetite, and he slept well.

Waiting for Results

Pasteur did not. The time when Joseph would develop rabies if the vaccine had not worked was approaching. The scientist's emotions swung between hope and fear. "Perhaps one of the great medical facts of the century is going to take place," he wrote to his son-in-law.[82] But, especially at night, the fear came back. What if the boy died?

Hope slowly won out. Joseph Meister was still healthy on July 27, almost a month after he had been bitten. Pasteur sent the boy and his mother back to Alsace. He told Joseph's mother to write often about how the child was doing. Month after month, Joseph showed no sign of illness.

Success and Failure

Pasteur reported Joseph Meister's treatment to the Academy of Sciences on October 26, 1885. The report caused a sensation that reached far beyond the academy. Physicians' opinions of what Pasteur had done were strongly divided. Vulpian, Pasteur's friend, proclaimed that by means of Pasteur's treatment "the development of hydrophobia can *infallibly* [unfailingly] be prevented in a patient recently bitten by a rabid dog."[83] This was an amazing statement to make after a single successful case. On the other hand, Emile Roux felt that Pasteur should not have treated a human being, or at least should not have published his work so soon. Roux, who had worked with Pasteur for many years, refused to work on the rabies project any longer. Most doctors withheld judgment until the results of more cases were known.

Ordinary people were less reserved. From all over France, people bitten by rabid dogs began to travel to Pasteur's laboratory. Many had no money and no place to stay. Making more vaccine and vaccinating and caring for these people became the laboratory's main task. Every bit of spare space filled up with rabbits, flasks, and patients.

The most disturbing of these early cases came to Pasteur on November 9, 1885. A ten-year-old girl named Louise Pelletier had been bitten on the head by a rabid mountain dog thirty-seven days before she reached the laboratory. Pasteur was sure that treating her was hopeless. Head wounds were the most likely to result in rabies. Furthermore, the girl had been bitten so long ago that she could be expected to show signs of the disease any day. He knew that if he vaccinated her and she died, his opponents would blame him for her death. Still, Louise's parents begged him to treat her. He felt he could not refuse.

Everything happened as Pasteur had feared. A few days after the last of her shots, Louise Pelletier showed the first signs of rabies. She died on December 2. Pasteur was by her side. His enemies publicized the girl's death widely. Some even claimed that Pasteur's shots had caused it.

Still the patients kept coming. Four poor children arrived from New York,

Pasteur examines a young English girl, one of the first patients he vaccinated against rabies.

their fares paid by donations. Nineteen peasants who had been attacked by a rabid wolf came from Russia. *Pasteur* was the only French word they knew. Other people poured in from Algeria, England, Germany, Hungary, Italy, and Spain, as well as from all parts of France. In March 1886, Pasteur reported to the Academy of Sciences that 350 people had been treated. Only one, Louise Pelletier, had died. By the end of the year, the number of successfully treated patients had grown to 2,500.

Support for Pasteur

In his March 1 report, Pasteur stated that "the prophylaxis [prevention] of hydropho-bia after a bite is established."[84] He asked that an institute be set up to produce and give the rabies vaccine. Scientists at the institute would also do further research on rabies and other diseases. The Academy of Sciences approved his idea. It began collecting money from France and abroad to pay for the institute's construction.

Still, the attacks against Pasteur continued. Jacques Grancher overheard another doctor shouting, "Pasteur is an assassin!"[85] The father of a child who had died after getting the vaccine threatened to sue Pasteur. People who objected to the use of animals in laboratories also criticized Pasteur's work. All these people had ammunition for their attacks because a few patients, like Louise Pelletier, died after arriving too late to be treated successfully. A few other patients became paralyzed.

Once word spread about the success of Pasteur's vaccine, patients arrived from all over the world to be treated by the famous scientist. Here, patients line up to receive the rabies vaccine.

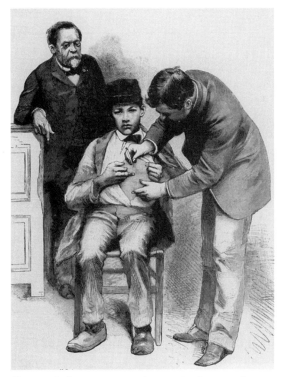

Pasteur looks on as an assistant vaccinates a boy infected with rabies.

The paralysis was caused by allergy to the nerve tissue in the vaccine. Pasteur's foes, however, called it "laboratory rabies."

Under this constant pressure, Pasteur's health began to suffer. He showed signs of heart trouble. "I did not know I had so many enemies," he said sadly.[86] Grancher, and even Roux, defended him as best they could.

Vital support for Pasteur's vaccine came from the report of a commission set up by the English government. The commission had been appointed in April 1886 to examine the new rabies treatment. In July 1887 the commission stated:

> It may . . . be considered as certain that M. Pasteur has discovered a prophylactic method against hydrophobia which may be compared with that of vaccination against small-pox. It would be difficult to overestimate the utility of this discovery.[87]

Actually it was easy to overestimate the usefulness of the discovery. Pasteur's critics were probably wrong in calling his treatment dangerous. However, it may not have been as effective as he believed. Many bitten people would not have developed rabies even if they were not treated. Nonetheless, the vaccine did—and does—save lives. It is the only way to prevent rabies in someone bitten by a rabid animal. There is still no cure for rabies.

Emile Roux stated that the rabies vaccine "increased the popularity of Pasteur more than all his former works."[88] It was an important discovery because it showed that vaccination could prevent or cure not only animal diseases, but also those of humans. It made a fitting end to Pasteur's scientific career.

9 Last Years

By the late 1880s, Pasteur was too ill to go on with his research. This fact was hard for him to face. Many honors came to him in his last years, but they eased his grief only slightly. Much greater comfort came from seeing younger scientists carry on his work.

The Pasteur Institute

Pasteur's dream of an institute where scientists could continue his work came true on November 14, 1888. An all-star group of friends, pupils, fellow scientists, and political leaders gathered in Paris that day to honor Pasteur and open the new Pasteur Institute. Money to build the institute had come in from all over Europe. Not only the French government, but the czar of Russia, the emperor of Brazil, and the sultan of Turkey had sent donations. So had ordinary people whose lives Pasteur had touched. One donation came from Joseph Meister. Rich and poor together raised 1,586,680 francs.

The new institute was an impressive stone building with large wings. The insti-

Donations were sent from all over the world to help construct the Pasteur Institute. The institute contained facilities for research, teaching, and medical treatment.

Pasteur's assistant vaccinates a child at the Pasteur Institute while others wait their turn (left). Pasteur's room in the institute has been preserved as a museum (right).

tute included facilities for making anthrax and rabies vaccines and treating rabies patients. It also had rooms for teaching students. Its large, up-to-date laboratories were ideal for research. Pasteur must have noticed how different they were from his first laboratory in the Ecole Normale's attic.

Pasteur himself, naturally, was the most important speaker at the dedication. A second stroke in October 1887 had weakened his voice. He therefore asked his son to read his speech. "It is now finished, this great building, of which it might be said that there is not a stone but what is the material sign of a generous thought," Jean-Baptiste said for his father.[89]

Pasteur and his wife moved into an apartment on the institute grounds. Each morning he visited the rabies clinic, arriving long before the patients. When people came to get their shots, he spoke to each by name. He dried the frightened children's tears. Later he went to the laborato-

ries where the rabies vaccine was being made. He checked on every detail of the process. He then went to the research laboratories to encourage the work of the scientists there.

The opening of the Pasteur Institute was not the only ceremony that honored Pasteur in his old age. The French government also prepared a grand celebration for the famous scientist's seventieth birthday. René Vallery-Radot described the beginning of this jubilee:

On the morning of December 27, 1892, the great theatre of the Sorbonne was filled. . . . At half past 10 o'clock, whilst the band of the Republican Guard played a triumphal march, Pasteur entered, leaning on the arm of the President of the Republic.[90]

Many speeches of admiration and gratitude were given. One of the most moving came from Joseph Lister. Lister was the

Pasteur is honored by the president of France and other admirers at a grand celebration on his seventieth birthday.

British surgeon who had used Pasteur's research as the basis for lifesaving changes in surgery and hospital care. Lister told Pasteur, "You have raised the veil which for centuries had covered infectious diseases. . . . Truly there does not exist in the whole world a person to whom medical science owes more than to you."[91]

Pasteur was pleased and touched by his worldwide fame. The progress made by his scientific heirs in their new laboratory, however, made him happier still. The greatest advance in the institute's early years was a vaccine for diphtheria. This disease, caused by bacteria, killed many children. The vaccine was first tested at the beginning of 1894. Before its use, one of every two children who caught diphtheria died of the disease. Within four months, the vaccine had reduced the figure to less than one in four.

A large conference to discuss the new vaccine was held at the Pasteur Institute on October 6, 1894. Vallery-Radot later described Pasteur's reactions:

> Pasteur, from his study window, was watching all this coming and going in his Institute. A twofold feeling was visible on his worn features: a sorrowing regret that his age now disarmed him for work, but also the satisfaction of feeling that his work was growing day by day, and that other investigators would, in a similar spirit, pursue the many researches which remained to be undertaken.[92]

On November 1, 1894, Pasteur suffered a severe attack of blood poisoning, caused by kidney failure. For two months he was very ill. After that, however, his health improved a bit. On June 13, 1895,

Pasteur spent his last days among his family. He poses with his granddaughter (below). France gave Pasteur a state funeral to honor his contributions to science (right).

he went to Villeneuve l'Etang, where kennels had been set up to house some of the stray dogs used in his rabies research. The dogs were now joined by horses, whose bodies were producing the lifesaving diphtheria vaccine.

The kennels and stables were in a beautiful park. Pasteur spent the summer days of 1895 sitting there under the trees. He watched the comings and goings of people and animals. His wife and daughter read to him. His two grandchildren often visited him as well. Vallery-Radot said that they "suggested young rose trees climbing around the trunk of a dying oak."[93]

By the last week in September, Pasteur could no longer leave his bed. He died on September 28, 1895, with one hand holding a crucifix and the other resting in Marie's. He was given a state funeral and buried in a magnificent tomb at the Pasteur Institute. Thousands of visitors come to the institute's chapel each year to see the tomb and honor this great scientist who did so much for humankind.

Pasteur's Ideas Today

Louis Pasteur contributed to many scientific fields. Scientists in all these fields are still exploring the lines of thinking that he began. Even more than practical tools such as pasteurization and the rabies vaccine, Pasteur's ideas are the heritage he left for the twentieth century. This epilogue describes ways in which some of Pasteur's ideas have been developed in modern times.

Chemistry

Pasteur founded the science of stereochemistry when he discovered, in his study of crystals, that the arrangement of atoms in a molecule could affect a substance's physical and chemical activity. Modern stereochemists have confirmed Pasteur's finding that living things often react differently to right-handed and left-handed molecules of the same chemical compound. Sometimes one form of a molecule is active as a drug, and the other is inactive. In other cases, one "mirror image" form of a drug is harmful. For example, a sleeping medicine called thalidomide caused tragedy in the early 1960s because it contained both right-handed and left-handed forms of a molecule. The right-

handed form produced the drug's desired effect. The left-handed form, however, caused pregnant women who took thalidomide to give birth to deformed babies. Scientists are now learning how to make

Pasteur sits peacefully in his garden in the last photo ever taken of him.

compounds with just one "handed" form. Thus, if a drug like thalidomide were invented today, scientists might be able to make a safe form of it.

Pasteur studied fermentation and other chemical processes by which microorganisms break down organic matter. He found ways to make fermentation more dependable and more useful to human beings.

People still use fermentation to make foods and beverages, just as they did in Pasteur's time. Scientists have also found other ways to use fermentation and other breakdown processes that microorganisms carry out. For example, certain molds and other microbes use fermentation to make substances that can kill other microbes. Some of these substances have been made into antibiotic drugs such as penicillin. Other microbes help people clean up the environment. Some microbes can break down oil, for instance, and are used to clean up oil spills.

Microbes

While Pasteur was trying to find out whether spontaneous generation occurred, he performed experiments to learn where microbes lived. These studies, along with his research on the way microorganisms broke down organic matter, gave him an appreciation of microorganisms' part in nature. René Dubos has pointed out that, unlike most people of his time, Pasteur realized that microbes play a vital role in recycling living and nonliving matter.

Today scientists know that microorganisms play many parts in the complex web of natural life. Some microbes live in the

Large tanks ferment wine at this Napa Valley, California, vineyard. Wine makers still use fermentation to make wine, just as they did in Pasteur's time.

roots of certain plants, such as peanuts and clover. These microbes change nitrogen from the air into a form that plants can use. Other microbes live in the stomachs of animals. They help the animals digest food. Discovery of these many roles bears out Pasteur's understanding that microbes play important and useful roles in our environment.

Pasteur once wrote, "A day will come, I am convinced, when microorganisms will be utilized in certain industrial operations on account of their ability to transform organic matter."[94] Today his prediction has come true. Scientists have learned how to modify microorganisms to make substances they could not make in nature. These one-celled factories make drugs, vitamins, and industrial chemicals. They can even make substances normally found only in the human body. Because the microbes can make large amounts of these substances, they cut the cost of factory processes and medical treatments.

In his silkworm studies, Pasteur pointed out that the overall health of the worms helped determine whether they would become sick when exposed to the microbes that caused *flacherie*. He recom-

mended preventing *flacherie* by providing plenty of air and space for the worms in the nurseries. These improvements in the worms' environment increased their resistance to disease. Keeping the worms healthy and strong, Pasteur said, was a better way of protecting them than trying to kill the disease microbes.

Doctors and other health care workers have learned that environment also affects human health. Poorly nourished children are more likely to catch germ-caused diseases than children who are well fed, for example. Breathing polluted air reduces resistance to lung diseases. A clean and healthful environment helps people as well as silkworms resist disease.

Tracing and Stopping the Spread of Disease

Pasteur, along with Robert Koch and other early microbiologists, worked out techniques for identifying the microbes that caused particular diseases. Pasteur used these techniques to identify the microbes that caused anthrax and childbirth fever.

Other scientists later discovered the microbes that caused other contagious diseases.

Pasteur and the scientists who followed him showed that different disease-causing microbes spread in different ways. Anthrax microbes spread from dead animals to soil, then to plants that living animals ate. The germs that caused childbirth fever were carried on doctors' dirty hands.

Once scientists knew which microbe caused a contagious disease and how it was spread, they could often find ways to stop the disease. Bubonic plague, for example, is carried by fleas that live on rats. People therefore learned to kill rats to keep plague from spreading. Today, scientists are trying to control the spread of AIDS by teaching people to avoid actions that can transmit the disease.

After Pasteur created vaccines for anthrax and rabies, people hoped that vaccines soon could be made for all major diseases caused by microbes. This did not happen for many years, though vaccines for most of these diseases do exist today. Many contagious diseases have been partly or completely controlled by vaccination programs.

Pasteur did not know why his vaccines worked. Today scientists know that vaccines help the body's immune system prepare to fight disease. The immune system is like an army that defends a country. It goes into action whenever a microbe or harmful substance enters the body. Some parts of the system can "remember" foreign materials they have previously encountered. If these materials reenter the body, the reaction against them is quicker and more effective than it was the first time. Vaccines work by introducing weakened microbes or their products into the body. This lets the immune system have experience with the microbes. Then, if full-strength microorganisms enter the body later, the immune system is better able to destroy them.

Pasteur's studies revealed ways to make fermentation more useful to humans. Today many of the antibiotic drugs we depend on are products of fermentation.

The Pasteur Institute

When Pasteur could no longer do research, he comforted himself by watching the scientists at the Pasteur Institute continue his work. The Pasteur Institute is still one of the world's most respected medical research organizations. It celebrated its

Improving Resistance to Infection

In an article titled "An Inadvertent Ecologist," René Dubos describes Pasteur's views about the role of health and environment in determining a person's resistance to disease.

"He took it for granted that the body in a state of normal . . . health exhibits a striking resistance to many types of microbial agents. As he pointed out, the body surfaces harbor various microorganisms that can cause damage only when the body is weakened. In contrast, infection often fails to take hold even when antiseptic measures are neglected in the course of surgery. Indeed, humans possess a remarkable ability to overcome . . . infection. . . .

Pasteur . . . accepted that resistance to tuberculosis [a serious lung disease caused by bacteria] was on the one hand an expression of hereditary endowment and on the other hand was influenced by the state of nutrition and by certain factors of the environment, including the climate.

In his words: 'A child is not likely to die of tuberculosis if he is raised under good nutritional and climatic conditions. . . . Let me emphasize that there is a fundamental difference between the characteristics that define a disease . . . and the set of circumstances that increase susceptibility to it [likelihood of getting it]. . . . There may be more similarity than appears at first sight between the factors that favor . . . tuberculosis and those that are responsible for the spread of the *flacherie* disease among silkworms.'. . .

This point of view naturally led Pasteur to conclude that resistance to infection could probably be increased by improving the physiological [health] state of the infected individual."

Pasteur believed that environment, as well as heredity, played an important role in determining a person's resistance to disease.

Robert Gallo of the National Institutes of Health (left) and Luc Montagnier of the Pasteur Institute (right) discovered the virus that causes AIDS. Researchers at the Pasteur Institute still search for a vaccine or cure for the disease.

hundredth anniversary in 1988. It started with a staff of fifteen scientists; today it has over five hundred. Pasteur Institute scientists have won at least five Nobel Prizes.

The Pasteur Institute is a leader in the study of diseases caused by microbes, just as it was in Pasteur's time. For example, it is deeply involved in research on AIDS. In 1983, Luc Montagnier and other scientists at the Pasteur Institute discovered the virus that causes AIDS. Robert Gallo and other scientists at the National Institutes of Health in the United States also found the virus at the same time. Shortly after-

ward, these two laboratories codeveloped a test to identify blood that has been exposed to the virus. Several Pasteur Institute scientists are now seeking a vaccine or cure for AIDS.

The Pasteur Institute is a fitting symbol for Louis Pasteur's work. Like Pasteur, it contributed to the science of the nineteenth century. Like his legacy of discoveries and ideas, it still contributes to science today. The Pasteur Institute reminds us that, one hundred years after his death, science still has much to learn from Louis Pasteur.

Notes

Introduction: Scientist of the Wonderful Century

1. René Dubos, *The Unseen World*. New York: Rockefeller Institute Press/Oxford University Press, 1962.
2. René Dubos, *Louis Pasteur: Free Lance of Science*. New York: Charles Scribner's Sons, 1976.
3. René Dubos, *Louis Pasteur*.
4. René Dubos, *Louis Pasteur*.
5. René Vallery-Radot, *The Life of Louis Pasteur*. Translated by Mrs. R.L. Devonshire. Garden City, NY: Garden City Publishing Co., Inc., 1927.
6. René Dubos, *Louis Pasteur*.
7. René Dubos, *Louis Pasteur*.
8. René Dubos, *Louis Pasteur*.
9. René Dubos, *Louis Pasteur*.
10. S.J. Holmes, *Louis Pasteur*. New York: Dover Publications, Inc., 1961.
11. René Vallery-Radot, *The Life of Pasteur*.
12. René Dubos, *Louis Pasteur*.
13. René Dubos, *Louis Pasteur*.
14. Emile Duclaux, *Pasteur: The History of a Mind*. Translated by Smith and Hedges. Metuchen, NJ: Scarecrow Reprint Corporation, 1973.
15. René Vallery-Radot, *The Life of Pasteur*.
16. René Vallery-Radot, *The Life of Pasteur*.

Chapter 1: The Tanner's Son

17. René Dubos, *Louis Pasteur*.
18. René Vallery-Radot, *The Life of Pasteur*.
19. René Vallery-Radot, *The Life of Pasteur*.
20. René Vallery-Radot, *The Life of Pasteur*.
21. René Vallery-Radot, *The Life of Pasteur*.
22. René Dubos, *Louis Pasteur*.

Chapter 2: Right-Handed and Left-Handed Crystals

23. René Vallery-Radot, *The Life of Pasteur*.
24. René Vallery-Radot, *The Life of Pasteur*.
25. René Dubos, *Louis Pasteur*.
26. René Dubos, *Louis Pasteur*.
27. Jacques Nicolle, *Louis Pasteur: A Master of Scientific Enquiry*. London: The Scientific Book Guild/Beaverbrook Newspapers Ltd., 1962.
28. René Vallery-Radot, *The Life of Pasteur*.
29. René Vallery-Radot, *The Life of Pasteur*.
30. René Vallery-Radot, *The Life of Pasteur*.
31. Jacques Nicolle, *Louis Pasteur*.
32. Louis Pasteur, "The Asymmetry of Naturally Occurring Organic Compounds," in *The Foundations of Stereo Chemistry: Memoirs by Pasteur, Van't Hoff, Lebel, and Wislicenus*. Edited and translated by George M. Richardson. New York: American Book Company, 1901.
33. René Vallery-Radot, *The Life of Pasteur*.

Chapter 3: Bubbling and Brewing

34. René Dubos, *Louis Pasteur*.
35. René Dubos, *Louis Pasteur*.
36. S.J. Holmes, *Louis Pasteur*.
37. René Vallery-Radot, *The Life of Pasteur*.
38. *Pasteur's Study of Fermentation*. Edited by James Bryant Conant. Cambridge, MA: Harvard University Press, 1952.
39. René Dubos, *Louis Pasteur*.
40. René Vallery-Radot, *The Life of Pasteur*.
41. Jacques Nicolle, *Louis Pasteur*.
42. Emile Duclaux, *Pasteur*.

Chapter 4: Where Do Germs Come From?

43. René Vallery-Radot, *The Life of Pasteur*.
44. S.J. Holmes, *Louis Pasteur*.

45. René Vallery-Radot, *The Life of Pasteur.*

46. *The Pasteur Fermentation Centennial 1857-1957: A Scientific Symposium.* New York: Chas. Pfizer & Co., 1958.

47. René Vallery-Radot, *The Life of Pasteur.*

48. Jacques Nicolle, *Louis Pasteur.*

Chapter 5: Savior of French Industry

49. S.J. Holmes, *Louis Pasteur.*

50. René Dubos, *Louis Pasteur.*

51. René Dubos, *Louis Pasteur.*

Chapter 6: Silkworms and War

52. René Vallery-Radot, *The Life of Pasteur.*

53. René Vallery-Radot, *The Life of Pasteur.*

54. René Vallery-Radot, *The Life of Pasteur.*

55. René Dubos, *Louis Pasteur.*

56. René Vallery-Radot, *The Life of Pasteur.*

57. René Vallery-Radot, *The Life of Pasteur.*

58. Emile Duclaux, *Pasteur.*

59. René Vallery-Radot, *The Life of Pasteur.*

60. René Vallery-Radot, *The Life of Pasteur.*

61. René Vallery-Radot, *The Life of Pasteur.*

62. René Vallery-Radot, *The Life of Pasteur.*

63. René Vallery-Radot, *The Life of Pasteur.*

64. René Dubos, *Louis Pasteur.*

65. René Vallery-Radot, *The Life of Pasteur.*

Chapter 7: Miracles on the Farm

66. René Dubos, *Louis Pasteur.*

67. René Vallery-Radot, *The Life of Pasteur.*

68. René Vallery-Radot, *The Life of Pasteur.*

69. René Vallery-Radot, *The Life of Pasteur.*

70. René Vallery-Radot, *The Life of Pasteur.*

71. René Dubos, *Louis Pasteur.*

72. René Vallery-Radot, *The Life of Pasteur.*

73. René Dubos, *Louis Pasteur.*

74. René Dubos, *Louis Pasteur.*

75. René Vallery-Radot, *The Life of Pasteur.*

76. René Vallery-Radot, *The Life of Pasteur.*

77. René Vallery-Radot, *The Life of Pasteur.*

78. René Vallery-Radot, *The Life of Pasteur.*

Chapter 8: The Conquest of Rabies

79. René Dubos, *Louis Pasteur.*

80. René Vallery-Radot, *The Life of Pasteur.*

81. René Dubos, *Louis Pasteur.*

82. René Vallery-Radot, *The Life of Pasteur.*

83. René Vallery-Radot, *The Life of Pasteur.*

84. René Vallery-Radot, *The Life of Pasteur.*

85. René Dubos, *Louis Pasteur.*

86. René Vallery-Radot, *The Life of Pasteur.*

87. René Vallery-Radot, *The Life of Pasteur.*

88. Emile Duclaux, *Pasteur.*

Chapter 9: Last Years

89. René Vallery-Radot, *The Life of Pasteur.*

90. René Vallery-Radot, *The Life of Pasteur.*

91. René Vallery-Radot, *The Life of Pasteur*; J.R. Porter, "Louis Pasteur Sesquicentennial (1822-1972)," *Science*, December 22, 1972.

92. René Vallery-Radot, *The Life of Pasteur.*

93. René Vallery-Radot, *The Life of Pasteur.*

Epilogue: Pasteur's Ideas Today

94. René Dubos, *Louis Pasteur.*

For Further Reading

M.D. Anderson, *Through the Microscope: Science Probes an Unseen World.* Garden City, NY: Natural History Press, 1965. An interesting account that describes microorganisms, their uses and dangers to human beings, and how scientists have learned about them. Includes information on Pasteur.

Paul De Kruif, *Microbe Hunters.* New York: Pocket Books, 1940. A lively book with a long chapter on Pasteur's research. De Kruif's account is sometimes more dramatic than accurate.

René Dubos, "An Inadvertent Ecologist," *Natural History,* March 1976. Discusses some of Pasteur's ideas that were ahead of his time, including his understanding of microorganisms' role in ecology and his recognition that environment is important in determining resistance to disease.

John Feltwell, *The Story of Silk.* New York: St. Martin's Press, 1990. A book on the development of the silk industry in China, France, England, and America. Includes a chapter on the life cycle of the silkworm moth, whose diseases Pasteur investigated.

Judson Gooding, "Pasteur's Progress," *Omni,* April 1988. An article about the Pasteur Institute on the hundredth anniversary of its founding.

Terence Monmaney and Diana Morgan, "The Bug Catalog"; Terence Monmaney, "Yeast at Work," *Science 85,* July/August 1985. Articles describing new uses to which scientists are putting microorganisms. Some microbes have become "one-celled factories" for making drugs and industrial chemicals, while others help to clean up the environment.

Don Nardo, *Germs.* San Diego, CA: Lucent Books, 1991. A book for young adults on microorganisms and how scientists have learned about them. Includes material on Pasteur.

Robert Reid, *Microbes and Men.* New York: Saturday Review Press/E.P. Dutton & Co., Inc., 1975. A lively description of how scientists have learned about microorganisms, with more biographical material on the scientists than most accounts. It has a chapter on Pasteur.

Additional Works Consulted

James Bryant Conant, ed., *Pasteur's Study of Fermentation*. Cambridge, MA: Harvard University Press, 1952. A collection of excerpts from Pasteur's major studies and speeches about fermentation, with explanatory notes.

René Dubos, *Louis Pasteur: Free Lance of Science*. New York: Charles Scribner's Sons, 1976. Perhaps the most readable adult biography of Pasteur. Sometimes difficult to follow because it is arranged by scientific subjects rather than by date.

René Dubos, *The Unseen World*. New York: Rockefeller Institute Press/Oxford University Press, 1962. Dubos's description of microorganisms and how scientists learned about them. Includes material on Pasteur.

Emile Duclaux, *Pasteur: The History of a Mind*. Translated by Smith and Hedges. Metuchen, NJ: Scarecrow Reprint Corporation, 1973. An account of Pasteur's scientific research, written by one of his associates. Fairly technical and difficult to read.

The Foundations of Stereo Chemistry: Memoirs by Pasteur, Van't Hoff, Lebel, and Wislicenus. Edited and translated by George M. Richardson. New York: American Book Company, 1901. A collection of papers and speeches by Pasteur and other founders of stereochemistry, the study of the way atoms are arranged in molecules. Includes two speeches in which Pasteur reviews his work on crystals.

Great Adventures in Medicine. Edited by Samuel Rapport and Helen Wright. New York: The Dial Press, 1961. Excerpts from the writings of scientists who have influenced medicine, including Leeuwenhoek, Lister, and Pasteur.

S.J. Holmes, *Louis Pasteur*. New York: Dover Publications, Inc., 1961. A relatively short, readable account of Pasteur's life and work.

"Institut Pasteur Begins Its Second Century," *Journal of the American Medical Association*, January 8, 1988. An article about the Pasteur Institute on the hundredth anniversary of its founding.

Bruno Latour, *The Pasteurization of France*. Translated by Alan Sheridan and John Law. Cambridge, MA: Harvard University Press, 1988. Describes Pasteur's position in the social movements of his time, such as the public health movement, and considers reasons why he had such an impact on nineteenth-century thinking. Latour thinks Pasteur's importance is somewhat overrated.

Elie Metchnikoff, *The Founders of Modern Medicine: Pasteur, Koch, Lister*. New York: Walden Publications, 1939. Metchnikoff, a Russian, came to work at the Pasteur Institute during the last years of Pasteur's life. His account focuses on Pasteur's importance to medicine and compares him to Koch and Lister, who also changed medicine in the late nineteenth century.

Jacques Nicolle, *Louis Pasteur: A Master of Scientific Enquiry*. London: The Scientific Book Guild/Beaverbrook Newspapers Ltd., 1962. Provides a relatively short and unusually clear description of Pasteur's scientific work.

The Pasteur Fermentation Centennial 1857-1957: A Scientific Symposium. New York: Chas. Pfizer & Co., Inc., 1958. A collection of papers that includes accounts of Pasteur's work on fermentation, a memoir by Pasteur's grandson, and articles describing modern uses of fermentation, including the making of antibiotic drugs.

J.R. Porter, "Louis Pasteur Sesquicentennial (1822-1972)," *Science*, December 22, 1972. A brief review of Pasteur's career and achievements.

Robert Reid, *Microbes and Men.* New York: Saturday Review Press/E.P. Dutton & Co., Inc., 1975. A lively description of how scientists have learned about microorganisms, with more biographical material on the scientists than most accounts. It has a chapter on Pasteur.

Karen F. Schmidt, "Mirror-Image Molecules," *Science News*, May 29, 1993. Presents modern developments in stereochemistry.

René Vallery-Radot, *The Life of Louis Pasteur.* Translated by Mrs. R.L. Devonshire. Garden City, NY: Garden City Publishing Company, Inc., 1927. Written by Pasteur's son-in-law, this book is the most important account of Pasteur's life. Focuses more on Pasteur's personal life than on his scientific work. Includes much interesting detail, but is long and somewhat hard to read.

Index

Credits

Cover photo by The Mansell Collection

Ann Ronan at Image Select, 40, 56, 65

The Bettmann Archive, 22, 77 (left)

© Tom Branch/Photo Researchers, Inc., 25

© Dr. J. Burgess/Science Photo Library, 20

© Jean-Loup Charmet/Science Photo Library, 68

Culver Pictures, 51

© Sylvain Grandadam/Photo Researchers, Inc., 82

Hulton Deutsch, 28, 38, 48, 54, 67

© Institut Pasteur, 12 (both), 15, 18 (both), 19, 21, 32, 41, 49, 52, 53, 57, 71, 74, 76, 77 (right), 79 (top), 80, 84

Library of Congress, 9, 13, 33, 42, 47, 58

© Will & Deni McIntyre/Photo Researchers, Inc., 83

The Mansell Collection, 29, 73

North Wind Picture Archives, 35, 44, 63, 69, 72, 75

Parke-Davis, 37, 60

Reuters/Bettmann, 85

© Earl Roberge/Photo Researchers, Inc., 30

Stock Montage/Historical Pictures, 16, 26, 27, 78

Permission to reprint quotations from the following copyrighted material is gratefully acknowledged: *Louis Pasteur: Free Lance of Science* by René Dubos, © 1950, 1976 by René Dubos. Reprinted with permission of Charles Scribner's Sons, an imprint of Macmillan Publishing Company. *The Life of Pasteur* by René Vallery-Radot, trans. by Mrs. R.L. Devonshire. Garden City, NY: Garden City Publishing Co., 1927.

About the Author

Lisa Yount's interest in science and biography began in childhood. Initially majoring in biology, she received a bachelor of arts degree (cum laude) in English and Creative Writing from Stanford University in 1966. As a freelance writer, she has worked on trade books, textbooks, and other educational material for young people for over twenty-five years. Her other books for young people include *Too Hot, Too Cold, Just Right* and *The Telescope* (Walker & Co.), *Cancer* (Lucent Books), and *Black Scientists* and *Contemporary Women Scientists* (Facts On File). She currently lives with her husband and four cats in El Cerrito, California.